Why the First World War Broke Out

Séan Lang

Searching finance

First published 2014 by Searching Finance Ltd, 8 Whitehall Road, London W7 2JE, UK

ISBN 978-1-90772087-1
Book design and typesetting by j-views, Kamakura, Japan

About the Author

DR SÉAN LANG is Senior Lecturer in History, specialising in the history of the British Empire. He obtained his PhD from Anglia Ruskin, focusing on the battle against maternal mortality in nineteenth-century British India, on which he has published. His interests in imperial history range widely, including the social history of empire, imperialism in popular and children's literature, and decolonisation. Séan has also published on nineteenth-century British political history and he is developing his research interests in the development of British constitutional identity from the sixteenth century onwards.

Dr Lang's career spans different sectors of education. He worked for many years in schools and colleges in Cambridge, including nine years as Head of History at Hills Road Sixth Form College in Cambridge. He was also Lecturer in Education at Exeter University for four years. He is Honorary Secretary of the Historical Association and has acted as adviser both to Government and to Opposition, as well as the Council of Europe, on issues related to history and history education. In 2005 he chaired the group that produced the Historical Association's important report on 'History 14-19'. He regularly speaks on matters relating to history on Radio 5 Live and on local radio. He has written textbooks and is joint editor of *Twentieth Century History Review* for which he writes regularly. He has written three works of popular history in the 'for Dummies' series.

Dr Lang is currently chair of The Better History Group; a small Think Tank of experienced history teachers and lecturers concerned to improve the current position and quality of history in the school curriculum.

About Searching Finance Ltd

SEARCHING FINANCE LTD is a dynamic new voice in history, business and economics. Our mission is to provide expert, highly relevant and actionable comment, information and analysis. We bring you the latest industry insight and best practice guidance, provided by writers who are renowned experts in their field, to give you the knowledge that will gain an edge for you and your organisation. To learn more, please visit www.searchingfinance.co.uk

Contents

Why the First World War broke out

Dr Seán Lang
Senior Lecturer in History
Anglia Ruskin University

For Alan Palmer
Historian, Teacher and Inspiration

Introduction

NINETEEN FOURTEEN. NOT EVEN ORWELL'S NINETEEN EIGHTY-FOUR can quite match it for evoking a sense of foreboding and doom. A century after it broke out, the First World War's hold on our collective imagination is as strong as ever. Remembrancetide in early November is heralded each year by the appearance of poppies in lapels and reaches its climax in the annual ceremony of Remembrance at the Cenotaph. Coach visits to the First World War cemeteries in Belgium and northern France are as popular as ever and feature in many schoolchildren's experience of history at school. In his last years Harry Patch (1898-2009), the last surviving British veteran of the war, became a celebrity, appearing frequently on television to speak of the futile waste the First World War had entailed. We are still haunted by the nightmare moonscape of the Western Front, by images of men blinded by gas, caught on barbed wire, mown down by machine guns or drowning in mud. The contrast between the horrors of the war and the lyric beauty with which they were described by the British war poets continues to fascinate us. The technology of the war – tanks, machine guns, gas, bombers, submarines – presaged all the features of twentieth-century warfare that later generations came to know only too well. This is the first war of our own era.

Yet, familiar though it seems in many ways, we are much less clear about what the Great War was actually *about*. It stands in sharp contrast to the Second World War, which we usually think of (not, let it be said, entirely accurately) as a war to stop the spread of Nazism. Since most people see Nazism as a uniquely evil creed, the Second World War, for all its many moral compromises and double standards, remains for most people a Just War: we know which sides were the 'Good Guys' and which the 'Bad'. No such certainty holds good for the First World War. Beyond a vague awareness that the Germans invaded Belgium (and even this is eclipsed in popular consciousness by the 1939 German invasion of Poland) few people nowadays could pinpoint exactly why Britain entered the war, and fewer still could say why the war needed to go on as long as it did. Any good the war might have achieved is heavily outweighed by the appalling conditions in which the soldiers had to fight and by the harm that was done by the Treaty of Versailles with which it ended. Since the Second World War owed its origins in large part to that treaty, it is no exaggeration to say that the Second World War was a legacy of the First, which in itself makes the 1914-18 conflict appear even more futile.

The manner in which the First World War broke out has long been the subject of satirical comment. *Oh! What a Lovely War!*, Joan Littlewood's celebrated 1964 Theatre Workshop production, later filmed by Richard Attenborough and still regularly performed in amateur productions, presented the outbreak of war in scathingly comic terms, as a falling-out among heavily caricatured national stereotypes. In the BBC TV satirical show *Blackadder Goes Forth,* Captain Blackadder gives a fairly accurate overview of the alliance system designed to prevent war breaking out in Europe but adds that this plan contained just one tiny flaw: 'It was bollocks'. Since satire has a way of settling in the memory more securely than the truth ever can, it is perhaps worth getting clear at the outset a rather more accurate outline of the events that resulted in a general European war breaking out in August 1914.

Why the First World War broke out

Outline of Events

BY THE 1870S EUROPE WAS DOMINATED by a small number of economically and militarily powerful nations known as Great Powers. These are usually identified as Germany, Great Britain, Russia, France, Italy, Austria-Hungary and the Ottoman Empire (Turkey). By and large, these powers enjoyed good relations with each other – by comparison with previous centuries, the nineteenth century was remarkably war-free and there was no equivalent of the terrifying international tensions of the Cold War era – but there were important areas of the globe where their interests clashed. The British and French were rivals in north and east Africa, the British and Russians in Central Asia, the Austrians and Russians in the Balkans. In addition, the process of creating a united Germany in 1871 had involved a war between the German states and France, in which the French had been heavily defeated in battle, Paris had been subjected to a long and destructive German siege, and two wealthy French provinces along the Rhine frontier, Alsace and Lorraine, had been annexed to the new German Empire. France therefore had a deep and long-standing grievance against the Germans and was committed to regaining possession of its lost territory.

To safeguard against any of these areas of tension provoking a war, the Great Powers established a set of alliances, which, after some re-jigging, had settled by the 1890s into two power blocs, a Triple Alliance between Germany, Austria-Hungary and Italy, and a bilateral alliance between France and Russia. Britain steered clear of a formal European alliance but did sign two *ententes* – a French word usually translated as 'understandings' – with France and Russia, in order to settle outstanding territorial issues in Africa and Central Asia. The entente with France also contained provisions for military co-operation between the two countries, though these were kept secret and their precise diplomatic implications remained unclear. These alliances and agreements provided a certain level of stability to European affairs, but they could not entirely wish international tensions away. Indeed, relations between Britain and Germany grew considerably more strained after 1898 when, under the direction of Admiral Tirpitz, Germany started to develop a major High Seas Fleet to challenge the supremacy of the Royal Navy. The British protested and began to increase their own naval building programme in what became a ruinously expensive Anglo-German naval arms race.

The years 1905-1914 saw a number of international crises, which are usually credited with having had the effect of increasing the tension between the Great Powers. This may be true, though international tension is not precisely measurable and does not in any case have to lead to war. In 1905 the German Kaiser challenged the growing French role in the nominally autonomous kingdom of Morocco; in 1908 Austria-Hungary annexed the twin Balkan provinces of Bosnia and Herzegovina, to the fury of the Russians and of the neighbouring state of Serbia, which had hoped to gain the territory for itself; in 1911 the Germans again challenged France's dominance in Morocco. These crises certainly helped to define and delineate the various alliances and agreements within Europe; in the two Moroccan crises, for example, the British stood much more solidly behind the French than might have been expected from the published terms of the *entente* between them. These crises did not, however, result in the outbreak of war. That arose out of the 1912-14 crisis in the Balkans.

In 1912 the Balkan states launched a war against the Turks to drive them out of this last remaining vestige of their European empire. The war was successful in that it left the Turks with only their capital, Constantinople, and some of the land in its immediate vicinity; however, the victorious Balkan states then quarrelled with each other over the division of the reconquered territory and the quarrel led in 1913 to a second Balkan War. The Great Powers were alarmed enough by the situation to impose their own settlement on the warring parties; however, one Balkan question, the situation in Bosnia-Herzegovina, remained unresolved.

Bosnia-Herzegovina lies at the northern end of the Balkans, to the north of Serbia and bordering the lands of Croatia and Hungary, which in 1914 were both part of the Dual Monarchy of Austria-Hungary. The provinces had a mixed population of Serbs, Muslim Bosniaks and Croats, and under international agreement, while remaining technically part of the Ottoman Empire they had been administered for the previous thirty years by the government of Austria-Hungary. The powerful Slav nationalist movement within Serbia had ambitions to annex Bosnia-Herzegovina as part of its plan to create a large Slav state under Serbian leadership; however in 1908 the government of Austria-Hungary, which had no desire whatever to see a large Slav state created on its southern border, formally annexed the provinces. Slav and Serb nationalists (the terms were to some extent the same) were enraged and hoped to reverse the annexation, by force if necessary. A Serb nationalist organisation called the 'Black Hand', many of whose members held high positions in the Serbian government, embarked on a campaign of violent agitation against the Austrians with the intention of rendering their continued occupation of the provinces too uncomfortable to maintain; the Black Hand's chosen method was political assassination. On 28 June, 1914 a group of Bosnian Serbs working in association with the Black Hand assassinated the Archduke Franz Ferdinand, heir to the Imperial and Royal throne of Austria-Hungary, during his visit to the Bosnian capital, Sarajevo. This act prompted the Austrians, after some diplomatic consultation with the Germans, to launch a war against Serbia, who then called for support to Russia, a fellow Slav state committed to support the Serbs.

There followed a period of intense diplomatic activity as diplomats sought to contain the conflict within the Balkan region and prevent it spreading into a general European war. In this they failed. The Russians stood by the Serbs and mobilised their army; the Germans, seeing the Russian mobilisation as a threat to themselves, mobilised their own army and launched an invasion of Belgium and France, as required by their war plan, the so-called Schlieffen Plan. This attack naturally brought Belgium and France into the war; the invasion of Belgium also prompted the British to declare war on Germany, since they were bound by treaty to defend the integrity of Belgium – as indeed were the Germans. Thus, by the end of the first week of August 1914, despite the best endeavours of most (though not all) of the statesmen dealing with it, a local crisis in the Balkans had led to a general European conflict in which all the major powers of Europe were at war with each other.

Was it inevitable?

IT IS OFTEN ASSUMED that once news of the assassination in Sarajevo was in the papers everyone across Europe immediately prepared for the war they knew would follow. This was not the case. That the assassination might cause *a* war – between Austria-Hungary and Serbia – was widely recognised, but that it might drag all of Europe into the biggest war since the defeat of Napoleon seemed not only unlikely but positively grotesque. The Balkan region had much the same reputation in 1914 for internecine violence and ethnic tensions with roots going back many centuries as it has today, and there seemed no ostensible reason why this assassination, shocking though it undoubtedly was, should provoke a war beyond the region's borders. Yet it did.

There was nothing new about high-profile assassination in Europe by 1914. The previous half century had seen assassinations of, among many others, a Tsar, Prime Minister and Interior Minister of Russia, no fewer than three American Presidents, and the Austro-Hungarian Empress: none of these had had widescale international repercussions and there was no obvious reason to think Franz Ferdinand's assassination would be any different. Far from its being a sort of lighted match applied to stockpiled timber, to use the sort of imagery still often employed, we need to be cautious about imagining a set of long-term 'causes' of the war at all. Obviously, some contributory factors in 1914, like the international alliance system, dated back thirty years or more, but seeing them simply as 'long-term causes of the First World War' is like arguing that some development in our own time is the *inevitable* cause of some as yet unknown event due to happen in or around the 2050s. Even if we accept that some statesmen definitely wanted a war and were actively preparing for it, and there is strong evidence of exactly that, it does not prove that the war that broke out in 1914 was unavoidable. Assassinations do not have to lead to war; neither do alliances, national rivalries or even high profile naval arms races. Moreover, the way in which events actually unfolded in 1914 did not go according to anyone's plan: even if the Germans and others were planning for a war, it certainly wasn't for the war they actually got.

The Great Powers

The Europe of the pre-1914 Great Powers looks strangely old-fashioned to modern eyes: its archdukes and emperors and elaborate military uniforms seem more like the fantasyland of Ruritania or a Lehar operetta than the most powerful and advanced region of the planet in the early years of the twentieth century. It was a world in which monarchy, even constitutional monarchy, was still regarded as the ultimate source of authority. Nevertheless, Britain, France, Italy and, to a lesser extent, the Austrian half of the Dual Monarchy, all operated a form of government clearly related to democracy as we would understand it today; Germany and Hungary had more authoritarian forms of government, though in each country the elected parliament played a crucial and increasingly important part in political affairs. Europe's most overtly autocratic state was Russia, where the Tsar exercised as close to absolute power as the pre-computer age allowed for. He was inevitably heavily dependent on his ministers and the civil service, or 'bureaucracy', and the Tsarist system also faced serious challenges from both constitutional and revolutionary groups, though, apart from some high-profile assassinations and a brief period of constitutional government after the 1905 revolution, their successes were as yet limited. The Russian autocracy in 1914 seemed as firmly entrenched as ever.

Economically the Europeans' strength, though unevenly spread through the continent, was unchallenged except for the rapidly developing economic might of the United States. The long-established industrial bases of Britain, Belgium and northern France had been joined by the rapidly growing industrial strength of Germany; Austria had developed a major industrial complex around Vienna, although the rest of the country remained rural; even Russia had developed concentrations of industrial production around Moscow and St Petersburg by the 1890s, thanks to the policies of the Finance Minister Sergei Witte. The European industrial economy was fed by Europe's world-wide network of colonies, which were milked for their raw materials. This process was not confined to the Great Powers: Belgium derived enormous profits from its possession of the Congo, an area many times bigger than it and rich in rubber, an essential product for the rapidly developing automobile industry. The main concentration of completely independent countries lay in the Americas, but even there the South American states were so heavily dependent on European investment and emigration that in effect they constituted an informal European (and mainly British) empire. The City of London had established itself by 1900 as the world financial capital, handling investments in colonial and quasi-colonial territories all over the globe.

This accumulation of industrial wealth demanded a social price: all the industrial cities of Europe and the United States saw their working populations living in conditions of poverty, squalor and disease which would appal even the most trenchant critic of the modern Welfare State. Britain and France were embarking on the slow process of developing a comprehensive system of state benefits, initially in the form of better housing and help with access to healthcare, and even Bismarck's Germany introduced a national insurance scheme in a vain attempt to stem the growth of socialism. Trade unionism was growing across Europe, including Russia, and by the 1900s unions were much more prepared than before to employ militant tactics, though only in France at the time of the Paris Commune in 1871 had there been a concerted attempt at a socialist coup, and that had been bloodily suppressed. Otherwise, despite the enormous extent of its working class population, industrial Europe was an increasingly middle class world.

Where once 'middle class' was confined to the wealthy industrialists, by 1900 the term encompassed a wide range of social groups, from impecunious but respectable office workers, through the aspirational middle managerial classes, to the much more exuberant wealth-displaying lifestyle of the ultra-rich. City life across Europe took on a more rigidly-set weekly routine than earlier ages had ever known: the early morning saw commuters – a late nineteenth-century phenomenon – rising, donning suitably presentable clothing, breakfasting and taking the new suburban trains, the newly-built underground railway or the newly-motorised omnibus into the centre of town to go to work; the early evening saw the same process in the opposite direction. On Sundays people of all classes donned their best clothes to go to church or chapel, perhaps with a walk in one of the newly-laid out municipal parks in the afternoon. Leisure time, indeed, was rapidly becoming an institutionalised part of the pattern of modern life: as well as the various public holidays and religious festivals, increasing numbers of Europeans, including the working classes, could afford to take some time out in the summer months to enjoy a stay at the seaside or in the country, while both cycling and motoring for pleasure were growing in popularity.

Despite the undoubted hardship of much working class life, apart from trade union strike activity Europe was surprisingly free of serious challenges to the existing social system. The most important political protest movement of the pre-1914 years was the British Suffragette movement, which saw women staging a mixture of eye-catching publicity stunts, militant public protest and violence against property. Yet even this campaign was a sort of back-handed tribute to the stability and prosperity of Edwardian society: far from challenging the parliamentary and monarchical British Constitution, the decidedly middle-class Suffragettes merely wished to be taken within its fold. A hundred years earlier working men in Britain had campaigned for the vote because they thought it an essential first step to pulling them out of poverty and the threat of starvation; the Suffragettes, many of whom fully intended to vote Conservative once they had won the right to do so, campaigned on the more abstract principle of equal rights and rigidly excluded any relation of their cause to socialist or revolutionary ideas. When the war broke out, Suffragettes proved some of its most rabidly patriotic supporters. For many years after the First World War it was common to hear the period before 1914 described as an idyllic Edwardian 'golden summer', a sun-kissed calm before the destructive storm of war; L.P. Hartley's novel *The Go-Between* is a good example. Historians have been challenging this image ever since George Dangerfield's lively 1935 study, *The Strange Death of Liberal England*, which portrayed the pre-1914 situation in Britain as a liberal society rapidly imploding in the face of militant trade unionists, suffragettes and Irish nationalists. However, just because a society is not enjoying a 'golden age' does not necessarily mean that it is on the brink of collapse. If material prosperity creates an illusion of security and permanence, which it certainly can do, it is easy to see why Europeans of the pre-1914 era could not envisage any circumstances in which their society and way of life was ever likely to end.

The Great Powers in Arms

GREAT POWER STATUS WAS GAUGED FIRST AND FOREMOST by military success. Military preparedness – the number of men in uniform and the planning and infrastructure that could deliver them quickly to where they would be needed – was an essential component of the Powers' international standing, but it could not substitute for success on the battlefield. A small state could gain international prestige by taking a minor part in a military campaign, even if it had no political connection with its causes: the north Italian state of Piedmont, for example, won much international respect by sending a contingent of men to fight alongside the British, French and Turks in the Crimean War (1854-6), even though the Piedmontese had no direct connection with any of the issues that had led to the war and few of their soldiers can have had any idea what the war was about (much the same could, of course, be said of the soldiers of the nations that were directly connected with the causes of the war). In similar fashion, various countries with no immediately obvious connection to the issues at stake would join in the First World War, including Portugal, Brazil and Japan.

All the major European states except Britain operated some form of conscription. This did not just mean having men under arms; after a period in uniform men served in the reserve, so the ability to call upon and deploy large numbers of reservists was crucial in preparing for war. Germany, which could call on some eight million reservists, had a major advantage here over its neighbours, France and Russia, whose military organisation was less well co-ordinated. Conscription had its origins in the French Revolution, which had created the idea of the 'Nation in Arms' to replace the haphazard recruiting drives and press gangs of the old regime, and the process had developed alongside the nineteenth century idea of the nation state. Military success was seen as the hallmark of a 'manly' people, and military service was central to the idea of the active citizen: A large army of citizens was, in effect, the mark of a modern state.

Germany was by far the best example of the link between nationhood and military success: it had forged itself into a unified nation through a series of successful wars fought between 1864 and 1871 under the direction of the Prussian Chancellor, Otto von Bismarck. The actual proclamation of the German Empire, which took place in the famous Hall of Mirrors in Versailles, had itself been the product of victory over the French in the war of 1870-1. Bismarck's victories had been achieved with a speed and crushing success that Europe had not witnessed since the days of Napoleon: the mighty Austrian Empire was decisively defeated in just six weeks in 1866 and, apart from the more protracted siege of Paris, France fell to the Germans in less than two months. The key to the Germans' remarkable success lay in the quality of their military planning, and, behind that, in a military mentality that often seemed to outside observers to permeate the whole of German society. The German army was run by a General Staff, a military administrative bureaucracy whose job was to prepare for war in any conceivable combination of military or geographical situations. This involved not just drawing arrows on maps, but working out the practical details of military infrastructure: which railway tracks were needed and where, how long station platforms needed to be, how many horses would be needed and where the grain would come from – and by what route – to feed them, as well as the military details of ammunition supply, trajectory of different calibres of gun and shell, the material needs of the men and so on.

Meticulous attention to detail paid off handsomely in Bismarck's wars, and other nations duly took note. Armies all over Europe upped their game in terms of proper military planning, factoring in the latest developments in transport, communications and weaponry, so that by 1914 all the Great Powers had some form of carefully worked out and calibrated plan for mobilising their armed forces and sending them into battle. These plans were by no means all of the same quality and there was still plenty of room for anachronism: the French army was still wedded to its colourful uniforms for battle and even the Germans retained their traditional *pickelhaube* spiked helmets. Nevertheless, the European Great Powers could go to war in 1914 confident in the belief that their army planning and organisation were as close as they could get to the state of the art.

How battle-hardened were these armies? Compared with their eighteenth-century predecessors, most nineteenth century European soldiers were much more likely to go through their army careers without ever hearing a shot fired in anger. The Austrian army, which had fought so often against Napoleon, undertook no major campaigns in the thirty-four years between his fall in 1814 and the outbreak of revolution in 1848, nor in the half-century between Austria's disastrous war with Prussia in 1866 and the outbreak of general war in 1914. After a period of intense military activity in the 1860s, the Germans undertook no major European campaigns after 1871, although they did deploy troops in their colonies. The French were active in North Africa but otherwise fought no major campaigns between their defeat in 1871 and the German invasion of 1914.

The two exceptions to this pattern of military inactivity were Britain and Russia. The Russian army invaded the Balkans in 1877 and undertook a major war against Japan in 1904. Neither war went well. The Russians made heavy weather of their 1877 campaign, where the Turks proved tougher in resistance to invasion than anyone had expected (a point that seems to have been forgotten when the allies contemplated the Gallipoli landings in 1915).

The Great Powers in Arms

The 1904 war against Japan was a disaster for the Russians both on land and at sea. In Napoleon's day, the looming power of Russia had overawed the leaders of Europe, but a hundred years later Russia appeared to be what Mao Zedong would later call the Atomic Bomb: a paper tiger, much less powerful than it looked.

Perhaps ironically, the army with the most continuous experience of active service belonged to the least militaristic of the Great Powers: Britain. Britain's small but highly professional army was deployed, often in fierce and difficult fighting, in British colonial territories all around the world. Colonial wars were by no means always the walkovers that modern commentators often assume: British military chiefs encountered determined and sometimes successful opposition in Zululand, Afghanistan, the Transvaal and Sudan. Troops stationed in India had their own 'wild west' in their endless skirmishing with the Pathans of the Northwest frontier. The longest and most hard-fought of the conflicts of the late nineteenth century was the Anglo-Boer War (1899-1902), in which the British suffered a number of humiliating reverses in the early stages before eventually retrieving the situation. During the guerrilla fighting that characterised the latter stages of the war, the British resorted to highly controversial counter-insurgency measures, including extensive use of barbed wire and the forcible detention of the civilian population in internment camps known (because they concentrated people in one area, where they could be supervised) as Concentration Camps.

With the exception of some of the fighting in the Russo-Japanese War (1904-5) and in the American Civil War (1861-5), none of this fighting mirrored the trench warfare that would dominate the First World War. This has led some historians to argue that the armies of 1914 were totally unprepared for the reality of modern warfare. It is certainly true that no-one involved in military planning before 1914 predicted that a future European war would consist largely of extensive trench warfare. The French army in 1914 didn't even wear camouflage colours: where the Germans wore 'battlefield grey' and the British khaki, the French went into battle in blue tunics and red trousers, their cavalry resplendent in shiny helmets and breastplates (the cadets at the military academy at St Cyr all vowed to wear their dress uniforms into battle, and did); with tragic inevitability these gorgeously-dressed French soldiers were mown down by German machine guns in the opening stages of the war. However, experience of colonial warfare was not as irrelevant to European conditions as is often assumed: it required imaginative improvisation in response to difficult terrain or conditions and it offered plenty of experience in storming defended positions, in the use of marksmen and sharpshooters, and even in the military use of barbed wire. Nevertheless, it is fair to say that the military prowess of the Great Powers before 1914 offered a dangerous paradox. The European states were militarised to a much greater degree than they had been earlier in the nineteenth century, yet, with the exception of the British, their experience of the reality of warfare was relatively limited. If it is true that experience of warfare cautions leaders against undertaking it too easily, the direct military experience of both political and military leaders in Europe in 1914 was worryingly small.

Was it a Militaristic Age?

WERE THE PRE-1914 EUROPEANS unusually violent or militaristic? Certainly, they were capable of shocking cruelty and violence, as their record in their colonial possessions illustrates only too graphically. The British systematically exterminated the native peoples of Tasmania and responded to the admittedly very violent Indian Mutiny and Uprising of 1857 with savage reprisals. The Germans set about the deliberate annihilation of the Herero people of South West Africa: the first attempted genocide of the twentieth century. The Belgians, who would be seen as the peace-loving, innocent victims of German aggression in 1914, instituted a veritable reign of terror during King Leopold II's rule in the Congo. If Europeans did not channel much of this capacity for violence into warfare among themselves, they were certainly developing a taste for the ceremonial trappings of war. Military uniforms were a far more common sight on the streets of European cities and at public and social occasions in the late nineteenth century than they had been a hundred years earlier. Monarchs usually presented themselves in military or naval uniform and so did some statesmen: Bismarck, for example, often wore military uniform even though he was a civilian. The cult of the military is often thought to have been delightfully encapsulated in an episode that took place in Berlin in 1906, when a trickster led the good citizens of the suburb of Köpenick a merry dance when he donned a captain's uniform and fooled them into obeying his ever-more outrageous commands without question. More serious was the incident at Zabern (Saverne) in Alsace, where in 1913 insolent behaviour by a German army officer came close to provoking a revolt across the whole province. Even without specific incidents, however, by the 1900s the military had become a familiar and influential factor in public life across the continent, and there grew a widespread tendency to normalise war, speaking of it airily as a sort of national exercise routine, a way of developing a physically healthy and active nation. Perhaps not surprisingly this equation of war with sport and physical exercise was particularly popular in sports-mad Britain.

None of this, however, can obscure the fact that by 1914 violence had largely been banished to the margins of European public life. The outbreaks of mob violence which had been so frequent a feature of eighteenth century city life had long disappeared. Of course riots could still break out, but when they did they were more isolated and unusual events. Rough or violent sports like football or boxing were now codified and conducted according to strictly enforced rules, a world away from their free-for-all origins. European wars were usually mercifully short and there was a much better recognition, at least in sober moments, of their cost. The short but bloody war between France and Austria in 1859 in northern Italy had shocked the Swiss Henry Dunant into founding the International Red Cross, which sought not merely to provide ambulance (ie mobile) medical care to the battlefield wounded but also, through the 1864 and 1906 Geneva Conventions, to lay down humane laws to protect the status of the wounded and of prisoners. In 1899 Tsar Nicholas II took the initiative in establishing the Hague Convention, which sought to substitute arbitration for warfare over territorial disputes, and banned some of the more dreadful latest developments in armaments, such as the dropping of bombs from balloons and the use of the soft-nosed dum dum bullet, which could eviscerate its victims. We are therefore presented with the paradox that the generation of statesmen and leaders who first sought seriously to limit the destructive effects of violence and warfare were also the generation responsible for producing the most destructive war in human history.

The Paralysing Fear of Defeat

POWERFUL THOUGH THEY APPEARED to the outside world, the European Great Powers were all to some degree haunted by fear. It was fear which dictated many of the fateful decisions of July 1914: fear of what would happen if Serbia were allowed to get away with the assassination, fear of what would happen if Russia did not stand by Serbia, fear of what would happen if Germany did not crush France quickly, and so on. But what were the Powers afraid *of?* The answer is threefold. Firstly, they feared loss of prestige; secondly, they feared the practical impact of defeat – loss of territory or draconian penalties; thirdly, they feared internal collapse. Their fears were well founded: by 1919, every single one of these outcomes had happened.

Loss of prestige is a nebulous but nevertheless real concept. Great Power status was entirely dependent on prestige – a country was a Great Power if others accepted and treated it *as* a Great Power. Thus Belgium had a huge empire in Central Africa but was too small to be regarded as a Great Power; Italy had a handful of not very profitable overseas possessions but was accepted as one. However, such acceptance was not necessarily permanent. Spain, Portugal, Holland, Poland and Sweden had all been Great Powers in their day, and in 1914 the first three still had overseas colonies, but none was regarded as a Great Power by 1900. Sweden and Holland's days of greatness were long gone; Poland had been partitioned between its neighbours; Portugal had suffered the indignity in the nineteenth century of actually being ruled from its overseas colony, Brazil; and Spain had recently lost what was left of its overseas empire in a disastrous war with the United States.

Anyone who thought that modern Great Powers were immune to that sort of decline needed only to look at the Ottoman Empire. A force to be reckoned with even in the eighteenth century, Turkey was so incapable of standing up for itself by 1878 that the Great Powers gathered in the Congress of Berlin to carve up its lands in the Balkans with hardly any reference to the Turks themselves. In 1908 a group of staunchly nationalist Turkish army officers known as the Young Turks seized control in a coup d'état and put in place a much stronger regime, but this new strength was not yet translated into military efficiency: the Turks were heavily defeated by the Italians in Tripoli in 1912 and comprehensively trounced by the Balkan states the same year.[1] By 1914 the Turks, who had once caused Christian Europe to tremble at their approach, had lost all but a toehold on the European continent and had completely lost control of North Africa: such was the awful warning to Europe of the consequences of losing prestige.

Less nebulous than loss of prestige was the impact of actual military defeat. Military defeat does not have to spell disaster: Britain recovered from defeat in the War of American Independence remarkably swiftly and France lost none of its international power and prestige after the fall of Napoleon (in more recent times, defeat in the Second World War certainly did not hinder the remarkable post-war recovery of West Germany and Japan). However, the Great Powers of 1914 had good reason to fear the impact of military defeat. Four of them, Austria, France, Turkey and Russia had recently known defeat and in each case it had cost them dear. Austria's defeat by the French and Italians in 1859 cost it the Italian province of Lombardy, and defeat by the Prussians in 1866 cost

---

1   The 'Young Turks' were formally the Committee of Union and Progress (CUP), but they are best known to history as the Young Turks.

Austria control of Germany, which had been in Habsburg hands since the 13th century. Although the Habsburg court continued to operate as the glittering centre of Europe, the plain fact was that Austria lacked either the means or the will to embark on war against any but the smallest states without substantial support from other European Great Powers. Military defeat had rendered Austria's very status as a Great Power open to question.

The Austrians were lucky that the peace settlement after their defeat in 1866 was fairly mild: no such relief was offered to the French when they had to surrender to the Germans in the Franco-Prussian War five years later. They were made to pay a large indemnity, to accept a German army of occupation until it was paid, and to hand over the immensely valuable border provinces of Alsace and Lorraine. In addition, the Germans staged a victory parade down the Champs Elysées and held the ceremony to inaugurate the new united German *Reich* in the famous Hall of Mirrors at Versailles. To get some idea of how humiliating this was for France, imagine the United States, after losing the Vietnam War, having to pay a huge fine to North Vietnam, accept a North Vietnamese army of occupation on its soil, hand over two entire states – say, Hawaii and California – to become Vietnamese provinces, and watch Vietnamese troops staging a victory parade down Pennsylvania Avenue before proclaiming reunification with the South in the Oval Office. No Great Power wanted to go through the national humiliation France had suffered in 1871.

The third consequence to be feared from military defeat was internal disintegration. There were plenty of examples of this happening. Within a year of Austria's defeat in 1866, the Hungarians had forced Vienna to concede Home Rule, dismantling the old Austrian Empire and establishing the Dual Monarchy, in which Hungary had equal status with Austria. France's defeat in 1871 led directly into the bloodbath of the Paris Commune and its suppression. Russia's defeat at Japanese hands in 1904-5 led to full-scale revolution. Fear of the consequences of defeat could never entirely eradicate the risk that the Europeans would go to war, but it did give an extra level of urgency to the search for a peaceful solution to political problems as they arose.

Was 1914 a Failure of International Relations?

THE WAR CLEARLY AROSE FROM A BREAKDOWN in European diplomacy. It is easy to characterise the foreign ministers and ambassadors of 1914 as heartless aristocrats, playing a sort of deadly board game with no regard for the suffering their machinations would produce (the diplomacy of 1914 has indeed been turned into a board game); however, this ignores the important point that European diplomacy before 1914 had in fact been highly successful in maintaining European peace. Diplomats and statesmen had been able to resolve some apparently highly dangerous conflicts, in the Balkans, in Africa, in South America, without their sliding into warfare; this is what made their complete and catastrophic failure in 1914 so bewildering. It is as if the spirit of Dickens's Mr Micawber had hovered over the statesmen of 1914, whispering in their ears that, while things might look very difficult, something would be sure to turn up.

Every generation has its 'powder kegs' – places or situations where the conflict of interests is so intense that it carries the risk of war. The 1910s generation was no exception, but it did seem to be proving capable of keeping these conflicts contained. The German annexation of Alsace and Lorraine, for example, is often cited as a dangerous provocation to the French; Bismarck himself saw it that way, which is why he opposed it. The French certainly kept the memory of the stolen provinces alive: in the Place de la Concorde in Paris the statues of Strasbourg and Metz, the capitals of the two provinces, were draped with chains as a perpetual reminder of their state of bondage. The idea that Germany was 'the Enemy' was taken for granted under the Third Republic (it was, for example, a central theme in the Dreyfus Affair) and the general desire for revenge even merited its own technical term, *revanchisme*. But it is very difficult to remain in a state of boiling rage for over forty years: long before 1914 the French had come to accept the reality of the annexation, rather as Germans in the 1970s and 1980s had come to accept the reality of the Berlin Wall, hoping it would come down one day but not expecting to see it happen in their lifetime.

Just as much as dismemberment, unification of a country could add fuel to international tensions. The unification of Italy by 1871 presented the world with the word *irredentism* for a particularly dangerous aspect of nationalist sentiment. The term comes from *Italia irredenta*, which is best translated as 'Italy with nothing left out': it expressed the wish to see all the lands that could possibly be counted as Italian reunited to the 'mother country'. In Italy's case, this meant Nice and Savoy in southern France; the Alpine Tyrol and the territory along the border with Austria-Hungary; and even the Adriatic coastline, which had once belonged to the maritime republic of Venice, although none of its people were now Italian. The idea that states should 'reclaim' peoples and territories which had once 'belonged', however tenuously or briefly, to their national group soon spread to other nationalities, notably the Poles and Serbs (later it would be the driving force behind Hitler's foreign policy) and would be a major factor in derailing the high hopes with which the victorious allies went into the negotiations for a peace settlement once the war was over.

Dangerous Colonial Conflicts

BY 1900, HOWEVER, THE CLASH OF INTERESTS which seemed most likely to provoke a war between the Great Powers was colonial conflict. Wars for imperial conquest had been closely tied to rivalries within Europe since at least the eighteenth century, and the danger that conflict in Africa or Asia might spark off war in Europe was as acute in the late nineteenth century as it had ever been. Until the 1880s the two main areas of potential clash were in central Asia, where Russian expansion towards the northwest frontier of India alarmed the British, and north Africa, where increasing British interest alarmed the French, who had long regarded the region as their own special sphere of interest. In 1882 Britain invaded Egypt and the subsequent French insistence that they too should expand their territorial holdings in North Africa in 'compensation' sparked off a general land-grab for African territory, both north and south of the Sahara, which was known even at the time by the unedifying soubriquet of 'the Scramble for Africa'. Although the land-grab was driven more by private entrepreneurs and buccaneers than by governments, international rivalry and suspicion were central to the process, especially once it became clear that the Germans intended to take part, taking land in west, east and southwest Africa for themselves. Bismarck hosted the 1884–5 Berlin Conference, which laid down an agreed process for laying claim to African land that would, it was hoped, limit the possibility of European war breaking out over African land-disputes, but the Europeans invested so much national pride in colonial expansion that it was simply not possible to remove all its potential for conflict. The most dangerous point was undoubtedly the 1898 Fashoda Crisis, which came close to plunging Britain and France into war over a stand-off at the small Sudanese town of Fashoda (now Kodok), of which, it is safe to aver, the overwhelming majority of people in either country had never heard. A French military expedition was crossing Africa from west to east, attempting to establish a French claim to an unbroken band of territory across the centre of the continent; a large British army had just defeated the Sudanese in battle and was establishing the title of the British-backed Khedive of Egypt to the whole of Sudan. Opinion in France against 'perfidious Albion' ran particularly high over British expansion in Africa anyway, and French public opinion was enraged by this new British interference, fuelled by angry newspaper editorials demanding war. Cooler heads in both governments managed to calm the situation, and ultimately it was the Fashoda war scare that prompted each country into the 1904 entente, but it was a sign not only of how easily colonial conflict could prompt calls for war, but also of the peculiarly strong reaction on the part of the French against any perceived attack on their position in what they regarded as 'their' African sphere of influence.

Other colonial conflicts actually did spill over into war. In 1898 war broke out between the United States and Spain after the mysterious destruction of the USS *Maine* in an explosion in the harbour of Havana, Cuba; the war saw the destruction of Spain's old empire and its absorption into the territories and sphere of influence of the United States. In the Anglo-Boer War (1899-1902) international opinion was firmly on the side of the two Boer Republics and Britain's colonial rivals at least contemplated the possibility of taking advantage of Britain's difficulties to move against British territory elsewhere. In the event Britain retrieved the war situation before any such move could be carried out, but the war had been a salutary lesson about the way in which colonial conflict could leave a European country vulnerable to its rivals.

In the 1900s, as Germany continued to build up its navy, the British, French and Russians patched up their differences in Africa and Central Asia in the two ententes, of 1904 and 1907. Nevertheless, the potential of colonial rivalry in Africa to provoke European tension was as strong as ever. The French, who regarded their Algerian lands across the Mediterranean from Marseilles as part of metropolitan France, were strengthening their hold over northwest Africa: they had established a Protectorate over Tunisia in 1881 (much to Italy's chagrin, who had her own ambitions in the region) and were gradually developing a similar arrangement in Morocco. So it was colonial rivalry which provided the Kaiser with an opening through which to challenge French control over Morocco, in order to see what support France could count on if matters came to confrontation. In the event, and perhaps unexpectedly, the strongest opposition to German interference in North Africa came from Britain, already concerned about the implications for imperial security of the massive growth in Germany's navy.

Colonial rivalry in North Africa also led, unexpectedly, to the crisis in the Balkans that was to serve as the actual spark to war in 1914. The Italians, keen to establish their credentials as a Great Power and resentful of the way the French were establishing their powerbase in North Africa (which the Italians, harking back to the days of Hannibal and Carthage, regarded as 'their' sphere of influence), launched an all-out attack in 1911 on the Turkish province of Tripoli, modern-day Libya. The Turks were caught off-guard and had difficulty reinforcing their small garrison because the Italian navy could attack them at sea while the British would not allow Turkish troops land transit across Egypt. Nevertheless, the Libyans and Turks inflicted a number of significant reverses on the Italians until the invaders were able to bring their superior technology to bear, including air power. The war dragged on into 1912 and the Italians, eager to bring it to a close, launched attacks against Turkish islands in the Aegean, occupying twelve of them (they became known as the Dodecanese, from *dodici*, the Italian word for twelve). This evidence of Turkish weakness offered a signal to those Balkan states wishing to challenge Turkey's dominance of the region, and in that sense therefore led directly into the sequence of Balkan crises that was to culminate in the Sarajevo crisis of July 1914.

The Anglo-German Naval Race

IT CAN BE DIFFICULT TO RECAPTURE NOW, after two world wars and years of footballing and political rivalry, but nineteenth-century Britain was actually strongly pro-German. There was an extensive German community in Victorian Britain, ranging from the royal family itself, which had been German since the Hanoverian Succession and under Victoria and Albert was rapidly becoming more so, down to an extensive community of German immigrants, often to be found in clerical work, teaching in public or grammar schools, or, further down the social scale, as shopkeepers, waiters or governesses.[2] A number of Germans had risen to prominent positions in British public life, like the chemist Ludwig Mond, the composer Felix Mendelssohn, or the banker Sir Ernest Cassell; Britain's nineteenth-century German community also included the political philosopher Karl Marx and his colleague, the wealthy industrialist Friedrich Engels. The Prussians had shared in the glory of Waterloo, the definitive British military victory throughout the nineteenth century, and Blücher, the name of the Prussian commander, was a popular choice of name in Britain for horses or

---

2   So common was it to find oneself served by a German waiter in London restaurants that British soldiers in the trenches used to enjoy calling out, 'Waiter!' to the German trenches. Germans who had lived and worked in England were usually fluent enough in colloquial English to shout back an appropriate reply.

steam engines. The British had good reason to fear the French and Russians at various points in the century, but they had nothing apparently to fear from any of the German states, who threatened neither the British mainland nor Britain's overseas colonies. The sudden emergence of Prussia as a military titan in the 1860s certainly caught the British by surprise and prompted them into a major rethink of their systems of education, training and military service, but there was no particular need for the British to feel threatened by the creation of an independent, unified Germany. In fact, Prince Albert had hoped that, through the link between the two countries' royal families, Britain and Germany could form a powerful European partnership.

That Britain and Germany fell out, despite the strong bodies of opinion in both countries in favour of closer ties, can be traced largely to the influence of two men: Kaiser Wilhelm II and Admiral Alfred von Tirpitz. Wilhelm was half English, through his mother, Princess Victoria, the eldest child of Queen Victoria and Prince Albert. His father, Crown Prince Friedrich, was staunchly anglophile and a great admirer of Britain's constitutional institutions; it was his intention, when he inherited the throne, to remodel Germany's constitution along British lines. Wilhelm – 'Willy' or 'Bill', as he was known in the family – was a frequent visitor to England from his childhood, spoke English fluently and took genuine pride in Britain's military and naval heritage. He was the proud possessor of a desk made from the wood of Nelson's *Victory* and he was delighted to have been given the honorary title of Admiral in the Royal Navy. He was devoted to Queen Victoria, his grandmother, and was at her side when she died; however, he also came to resent his parents' assumption that English ways were invariably superior to German. His rebellion against his parents' values was encouraged by Bismarck, a rare exception among Germany's otherwise anglophile political establishment, and later by his wife, Dora, who could not stand the English. When he came to the throne Wilhelm set out, not unlike a modern teenager rebelling against his parents, to

establish his independence of action by acts which were either cal-
culated to cause offence in Britain or – perhaps worse – were not
intended to offend but did. In 1895 he sparked a major and quite
unnecessary diplomatic spat with Britain by sending a telegram of
congratulation to President Paul Kruger of the Transvaal Republic on the defeat of the Jameson Raid, a madcap British attempt
at sparking a revolt among the Transvaal's immigrant population.
In 1908 Wilhelm gave a disastrous interview to the *Daily Telegraph*
in which he called the English mad for not realising he was their
friend, not their enemy, and suggested that it was only thanks to
his own efforts that Britain had won the Anglo-Boer War without
having to face intervention by the French and Russians. Quite
apart from the outrage his words caused in Paris and St Petersburg,
the interview revealed a breezy tactlessness and lack of diplomatic finesse that caused almost as much embarrassment in Berlin as
it caused outrage in London. The Kaiser soon became a sort of
bogeyman for the British press and it proved easy during the war
for British propaganda to pin on him all the imagined evils of the
German war machine itself.

The Kaiser's dangerous cocktail of admiration and resentment,
love and hate for the British was epitomised in his pet project, to
build up a German fleet to rival the power and stature of the Royal
Navy. Though one could be forgiven for thinking so, there was in
fact no law in the nineteenth century that laid down that only Britain was allowed to maintain a large, world-class fleet. Nevertheless,
global British naval superiority had been an accepted fact of international life since Trafalgar, and since 1889 it had been officially
adopted as British policy under the 'two-power standard', a rule-
of-thumb criterion by which the British committed themselves to
maintaining a fleet at least as large as those of the next two largest
powers' combined. The two Powers the British had in mind were
France and Russia, though the United States was also making important progress, especially in warship design. It was an American
admiral, A.T. Mahan, who argued in 1890 in *The Influence of Sea*

Power in History that Napoleon's failure to mount an effective challenge to British naval supremacy had been the ultimate cause of his downfall, and that naval power was the key to Great Power status. Mahan's argument, which was eagerly devoured in Berlin, was all the more relevant because naval design had undergone a revolution since Nelson's day which opened command of the sea to any nation with the technological know-how – and the money – to build a modern fleet.

The sailing ships of Nelson's day had given way first to steam power, a transition ruefully captured in Turner's painting *The Fighting Temeraire*, and then to the development of ironclad warships. France launched the first of these, *La Gloire*, in 1859; Britain followed in 1860 with HMS *Warrior*. With changes in ship design came major changes in gunnery: out went the old cannons, each individually aimed on its own trolley; in came much heavier guns firing high explosive shells, able to swivel their turrets, and with sophisticated aiming devices which could pinpoint an enemy ship from huge distances, taking account of its speed and direction. A sign of the future was the celebrated action in 1862 during the American Civil War between the Confederate ironclad *Merrimack* (fighting as the CSS *Virginia*) and the USS *Monitor*, an exchange of fire between two metal monsters that would have bewildered Nelson a mere generation earlier.

These changes in naval design and gunnery meant that the British could not afford to rest on their Nelsonian laurels. They had to develop a fleet of ironclad steamships and acquire the worldwide network of coaling stations needed to fuel them. They were still conscious of the need to outbuild the French and Russians, but since neither country showed signs of mounting a serious challenge to Britain's naval superiority the British could afford to take their supremacy for granted. That sense of security ended, however, when Tirpitz was appointed Secretary of the Imperial German Navy Office, the equivalent of Britain's First Lord of the Admiralty, in 1897.

Tirpitz's appointment was part of a shift in German foreign and colonial policy towards *Weltpolitik*, the idea that Germany should operate as a global power with interests in all parts of the world. It provided the context for Germany's drive for colonial possessions in Africa, in China and in the Pacific; it also required the establishment of a substantial fleet, and to this end Tirpitz sponsored two Navy Bills submitted to the Reichstag in 1898 and 1900, authorising a huge increase in Germany's battleships and cruisers. Such a sudden change in policy was bound to provoke surprise in Britain; the anti-British rhetoric that accompanied it turned that surprise into alarm. Major armaments programmes are always phenomenally expensive, and any government will only usually underwrite one if it can be sure that it will enjoy public support. The taxpayer, then as now, will only support heavy defence spending if it is plausibly directed against a clear and identifiable threat. Tirpitz could only justify spending vast sums of money to expand the German fleet, with inevitable consequences for public spending in other areas, if the German public were convinced that Britain constituted such a threat; since Britain didn't, it was necessary to concoct a huge anti-British bogey scare to persuade the Germans that it did. So the expansion of the German fleet was justified on the grounds that Britain, for its own nefarious and selfish reasons, was preventing Germany from establishing the empire which was its by inviolable right – Germany's 'place in the sun', as the phrase went. The more virulent the anti-British propaganda that poured off German presses, the more alarmed the British were and the more ready the British public was, in turn, to pay for the expansion of the Royal Navy in response, so that by the 1900s the two countries were locked in a ruinously expensive naval building race. To fuel anti-German feeling still further, the British developed a taste for a whole new genre of outlandish spy stories, like William Le Queux's *Spies of the Kaiser* (1909), Saki's *When William Came* (1914) or the most famous, Erskine Childers's *The Riddle of the Sands* (1903), which portrayed the Germans as a fiendishly clever people, addicted to their dreams

The Anglo-German Naval Race

of world conquest, which usually began with a mass descent of thousands of German troops on the southern coast of England.

Tirpitz knew he could not hope to outbuild the British; instead his aim was to create a 'risk fleet', one that could do enough damage to leave the British vulnerable to the French and Russians, their two-power standard in tatters. It was in many ways a sensible strategy, given the imbalance between the two countries' fleets; however, in the early years of the twentieth century a series of diplomatic and political development tilted the balance of advantage back in Britain's favour. In 1902 Britain signed an alliance with Japan which handed responsibility for protecting British interests in Asia to the Japanese and freed the Royal Navy to concentrate its forces closer to home. In 1903 the British created a special North Sea fleet based at Rosyth, from where it could quickly deploy against the Germans. Tirpitz's hopes of wrecking Britain's two-power standard were dealt a serious blow by the 1904 Anglo-French entente, which removed any remaining threat from France and allowed Britain to concentrate on maintaining its margin over Germany. In the same year, the dynamic Sir John 'Jacky' Fisher was appointed First Sea Lord, the professional head of the Royal Navy, and set about a systematic programme of modernisation, scrapping obsolete models of ship without a trace of sentimentality and concentrating on building enough of the right types of ships, rather than worrying about the total number of vessels. He oversaw the move from steam power to diesel, ending the navy's reliance on far-flung coaling stations. He was particularly keen on the battlecruiser, a fast-moving but lightly-armoured vessel that could act as a hunter for the main fleet, seeking out the enemy and dealing with any but the largest ships. And then in 1905, a year after he was appointed, the game changed. Britain launched HMS *Dreadnought*.

Normally a battleship can have either speed or weight of armament; *Dreadnought* had both. Its turbine engines gave it a top speed of 21 knots, two or three knots faster than other battleships; it was fitted with 11-inch guns, whereas most battleships had nothing bigger than 9-inch. It is often said that *Dreadnought* rendered all existing ships obsolete, and it did; this one model of battleship rendered almost all Britain's fighting fleet redundant at a stroke. The game was now open to anyone willing to put up the money to build enough of the new type of battleship. The Anglo-German naval race was on in earnest.

Britain won the race for dreadnoughts, as it was always likely to. By the 1910s ever-larger dreadnoughts were rolling off the slipways, with bigger guns and capable of even greater speed, and the German government was finally balking at the ever-rising cost; the German army was complaining that too much money was being diverted from its needs to meet the requirements of the navy. When war actually came, the most effective vessels Germany deployed were the small commerce raider and the submarine, neither of which had featured in the naval race at all. However, the naval race played a crucial role in creating the atmosphere that produced war in 1914. Almost single-handedly, it created a deep sense of mutual suspicion and resentment between the British and the Germans that simply had not existed before and might very well not otherwise have done. Germany was the only European country that late nineteenth-century Britain approached with a view to a possible alliance and many German diplomats and statesmen still regretted that this had not proved possible; the rhetoric of contempt and suspicion that accompanied the naval building programme in both countries rendered such a partnership unthinkable. Secondly, the naval race revealed to British statesmen how vulnerable Britain was to attack and the hollowness of the illusion that Britain did not need European partners. To help meet the German challenge, in 1912 the British and French signed a naval agreement whereby the British withdrew their fleet from the Mediterranean and concentrated their strength in the Channel and the North Sea: France withdrew its fleet from its northern and Atlantic coasts and concentrated it entirely in the Mediterranean, Britain undertaking to defend France's Channel and Atlantic coasts. This was to have important consequences two years later.

Conflict in the Balkans

THERE IS TENDENCY AMONG WESTERNERS when the Balkans are mentioned simply to throw up one's hands in despair, as if years of ethnic and religious tensions are endemic to the region, imbibed by the region's children with their mothers' milk. This attitude will not do when it comes to understanding in any sort of depth the chain of events that led to European war in 1914. What made the Balkan region such a uniquely dangerous region in the 1910s?

Western Europeans often have difficulty understanding the Balkan region because, although it has long played its part in the history of the continent as a whole, the region can still seem irredeemably 'different' from the norms with which westerners are familiar. It uses different alphabets from western Europe and follows different religious traditions: it is home to Europe's longest-resident indigenous Muslim population and even its Christian tradition is Orthodox rather than Catholic. For many years the western Catholic Church regarded Orthodox Christians with suspicion, and the medieval crusaders viewed their fellow-religionists as little better than the Saracens they had travelled east to fight. The only major power which could claim to have more similarities than differences with the Balkan peoples was Russia, which, for western Europe, merely added to the region's danger: by the nineteenth century any Great Power with reason to fear Russian expansion (and they all had at one point or another) tended to regard the Balkan peoples as little more than Russian stooges.

The biggest block to a Russian takeover of the Balkans was the fact that the region was ruled by the Ottoman Turks, but by the eighteenth century the Ottomans' days of greatness were far behind them. They were engaged in a long, slow process of decline while their neighbours, the Russian and Habsburg empires, expanded their own frontiers into what had been Ottoman territory. In addition, Russia established its right by treaty to interfere in the internal affairs of the Ottoman Empire in order to protect the interests (and sometimes even the lives) of the Empire's Orthodox Christian subjects. To this gradual process of Turkish decline the French Revolution added the fashionable and potentially explosive ingredient of Nationalism, which proved highly attractive to the different Balkan peoples, eager to revive the glory days of their pasts. First the Serbs, during the Napoleonic Wars, and then the Greeks shortly afterwards, rose in rebellion against the Turks, attracting considerable fashionable sympathy and support both in Russia, where it was only to be expected, and also in western Europe, which always tended to take other people's nationalist rebels to its heart. Thanks to western military intervention, Greece was established in independent, if truncated, form in the 1820s; Serbia took longer to establish its own autonomy but was largely self-governing from 1867: A precedent had been set for the eventual collapse of Turkey's empire in the Balkans. In a much-quoted phrase, Tsar Nicholas I is supposed to have referred to the Ottoman Empire as a 'sick man', whose estate would soon need to be divided up by the other European powers: the most contentious area of that estate was unquestionably the Balkans.

Balkan nationalism took a significantly different form from nationalism in other parts of Europe. Most European nationalists believed in the 'big' nation, into which smaller countries and loyalties should be subsumed: Germans or Italians were called upon to drop their regional identities and take pride in their new national

identity. The equivalent in the Balkans was the phenomenon of
'Pan-Slavism', the belief in a large Slav state that would encompass
all the Slavic peoples of the southern Europe. It was generally assumed that Serbia would play the same leading role in the creation
of this Pan-Slav state that Piedmont had played in Italy and Prussia
in Germany. However, at the same time as Pan-Slav identity was
gathering pace, the Balkan peoples retained and even strengthened
their own separate senses of national identity, as Greeks, Bulgarians,
Romanians and so on. This particularist form of Balkan nationalism meant that attempts to set a pan-Slavic movement in motion
were continually frustrated by quarrels between the different Balkan
peoples, usually over territory. Moreover, since any sort of nationalist movement would have to confront the Austrian and Turkish
empires that dominated the region, all Balkan nationalists, whether
Pan-Slavic or particularist, would need to turn to the Russians for
support. That in turn aroused the suspicions of the western Powers,
who feared, not without reason, that the Russians hoped to use
their influence in the region to secure access to the warm waters of
the Mediterranean for their fleet. This could significantly alter the
balance of European politics and was therefore strongly resisted by
London and Paris, and sometimes Vienna and Berlin as well. The
future of the Balkans was therefore an issue of the first international
importance and Balkan nationalism was subject to international
intervention to a much greater degree than had been the case in
Germany and Italy.

The fate of Bulgaria in the 1870s perfectly illustrates the prob-
lem. In 1875, following the successful example of the Serbs and
Greeks, the Bulgarians staged a national rebellion to win their independence from the Turks. The Turks responded with slaughter
and mutilation that shocked opinion across Europe, setting a pattern of atrocity in the region that would be repeated at intervals
right down to the killing which ravaged Bosnia in the 1990s. In
1877, to international alarm though to no-one's great surprise, the
Russians sent an army into the area to help their fellow Slavs and,

after eventually overcoming surprisingly stiff Turkish resistance, the Russians were able to force the Turks to sign the Treaty of San Stefano, a settlement which worked massively to the advantage of the Bulgarians and the Russians themselves. San Stefano created a large independent Bulgarian state that reached over to the Aegean coastline, and would almost certainly prove a grateful and loyal Russian client: in effect, Russia had extended its own borders across to the Mediterranean. This generous territorial settlement alarmed Bulgaria's neighbours, who saw large areas of what they regarded as 'their' land being given to the new state; more importantly, it alarmed the Great Powers, especially Britain, which rushed its armed forces to the region and threatened the Russians with war if they did not agree to an international congress to rescind the Treaty of San Stefano and impose its own settlement on the region. The Russians, with no major state supporting them, backed down and the international congress was duly held in Berlin, chaired by the German Chancellor, Bismarck, who claimed, somewhat disingenuously, to be acting as a strictly neutral 'honest broker' between the Russians and the British. The Congress of Berlin resolved the stand-off in terms highly acceptable to Britain: Bulgaria was cut in three and pushed well back from the Aegean; Serbia, Romania and Montenegro, which had all enjoyed a degree of autonomy within the Ottoman Empire, became fully independent states and, in a rather clumsy arrangement, the administration of Bosnia-Herzegovina was given to Austria–Hungary, though it remained within the Ottoman Empire.

In every way except its outcome, this 1877-78 crisis was, if anything, a *more* serious threat to European peace than the 1914 crisis: the Russian invasion of the Ottoman Empire and the creation of a large Bulgarian puppet state (or so the west regarded it) was a direct challenge by a major Power to the diplomatic status quo in this highly sensitive region, in a way that the assassination of Franz Ferdinand was not. Moreover, Britain's robust response left the Russians very little room for any sort of face-saving compromise:

had the Congress of Berlin failed, the continent was facing a major European conflict.[3] Yet the Powers were able to resolve the 1877-78 Balkans crisis without resort to war in a way they proved totally incapable of replicating in 1914. Why? The answer lies in four key differences:

a) In 1877-8 all the other Great Powers largely supported the British: they were not tied into a system of opposing alliances in which any power felt obliged to support its ally regardless of the merits of the actual issue.

b) No-one in 1914 was able to play the equivalent of Bismarck's role in 1878 as an acceptable peacebroker to both sides, though Sir Edward Grey, the British Foreign Secretary did try to.

c) In 1878 the Great Powers were prepared to entrust their fortunes to an international congress of heads of government rather than insisting on mobilization and war to defend their own interests and advantage, as they were to do in 1914.

d) In 1877-8 Britain moved decisively and fast, leaving no room for misinterpretation of its wishes and intentions; in 1914, by contrast, European statesmen and diplomats spent much of their time speculating about what each state's intentions were, in what precise circumstances they would definitely go to war and in what circumstances they would accept a different outcome, all of which, fatally, provided ample space for misunderstanding and confusion.

In other words, the Bulgarian crisis of 1875-8 provided a clear precedent for the statesmen of 1914 of how to resolve a Balkan crisis, but it was a precedent that the Powers chose not to follow. Equally, 1875-8 provided an object lesson in how international politics could scupper even the most fervent nationalist movement in the Balkan region. To this day, Bulgarians remember the 1875-8

---

3   This was the crisis that produced the famous music hall song proclaiming that 'we don't want to fight, but by jingo! if we do, We've got the men, we've got the ships, we've got the money too!', which in turn gave the word 'jingoism' to mean aggressive patriotism.

crisis as one in which their national aspirations were frustrated by western self-interest. In the short term it meant that Balkan nationalists, whether particularist or Pan-Slavic, were up against a series of blocks which, even with Russian help, they would have great difficulty in overcoming: the Turks, the Austrians, and the western Great Powers. For the two decades that followed, therefore, Slav nationalism remained an unattainable dream until, in the new century, the situation was changed in a very short space of time by three events: two unexpected changes of regime and one alarming change of policy. The changes of regime took place in Serbia and Turkey, the change of policy in Austria-Hungary.

New Regime in Serbia

In 1903 a particularly bloody coup d'état was staged in the Serbian capital Belgrade, in which the King and Queen were hunted down in the royal palace and hacked to pieces. King Alexander had been an increasingly erratic and autocratic ruler but he had been pragmatic enough to recognise that Serbia was in a weak position and would be well advised to establish good relations with its powerful neighbour, Austria–Hungary; it was this policy, which went against all the instincts of Serb nationalists, that sealed his death warrant. The assassins were led by a ruthless Serbian nationalist officer, Colonel Dragutin Dimitrević, who bore the codename 'Apis' after a supposed resemblance to the physique of the Egyptian god of that name. Apis masterminded the transfer of the throne to the elderly King Peter I of the rival house of Karadjordjević; the new king was much more prepared than his predecessor to take a strongly anti–Austrian line. 'Apis', who headed Serbia's secret services, went on in 1911 to found the Black Hand, a terrorist group dedicated to assassination, especially of prominent figures in the Austro–Hungarian hierarchy. Its track record was not, in fact, particularly good: the Black Hand had tried and failed to kill both the Emperor Franz Josef and the Austrian Governor of Bosnia-Herzegovina, General Oskar Potiorek; the plan to assassinate the Archduke Franz Ferdinand was a sort of 'third time lucky'.[4] Nevertheless, Apis remained

---

4   Potiorek, who went on to command Austrian troops in the First

a powerful figure in the Serbian government, with considerable political and military support and able to operate apparently beyond
any form of control.

World War, was probably the luckiest of the Black Hand's intended victims. He was riding with the Archduke in the car on 28th June 1914 and
Princip, who was firing at point-blank range, tried to shoot him as well;
instead he killed the Archduchess.

Why the First World War broke out

Turkey: the Sick Man gets out of bed

WHILE SERBIA WAS PREPARING ITSELF to stand up to one of its powerful neighbours, the other, the Ottoman Empire, was undergoing its own momentous political change. In 1908 a strongly nationalist group of officers, known as the Young Turks, staged a coup in Constantinople and started to inject a bit of backbone into the 'Sick Man of Europe'. The Turks had, in fact, been flexing their muscles for some years before and were showing increasing signs of irritation with their traditional allies, the British and French. In the 1890s Sultan Abdul Hamid II, known in the west as 'Abdul the Damned', authorised wholesale massacres of the empire's Armenian population, who had been demanding similar concessions as those made to the empire's various national groups in the Balkans. A nationalist rising on Crete in 1896 was crushed with similar ruthlessness. By the 1890s liberal opinion in the west, and particularly in Britain – the Armenian massacres were the subject of Gladstone's last political campaign – was increasingly disgusted by the evidence of the Ottoman regime's contempt for human life and its refusal to change. At the same time, the Turks, tired of being lectured by their western protectors, started to flirt with the Germans: in 1898 Kaiser Wilhelm II made a successful state visit to Turkey and to Jerusalem and in 1903 the Turkish government granted a German-backed company permission to build the key railway line to Baghdad. Since the Kaiser refrained from making any criticism of his hosts' style of rule, it seemed to the Turks that they had found a very acceptable alternative ally who had the advantage firstly of being able to threaten Russia directly, if necessary, and secondly of not forever preaching at the Turks for falling short of western norms of ethical behaviour.

Not surprisingly, perhaps, the German-Turkish relationship soon showed signs of strain: the Turks came to resent the way their new German friends treated them as a German puppet state: the 1908 Young Turks coup was largely intended to restore Turkey's independence of action. Rather like the Japanese, the Young Turks realised that their empire's only hope of flourishing in the twentieth century lay in adopting as much as it dared of western culture and technology. In 1909 the Young Turks replaced Abdul Hamid II with the more pliable Mehmet II and instituted a campaign to reform Turkish society along western lines. They were less successful in this than the Japanese had been: conservatism in Turkish society was too strong even for the Young Turks to overcome as quickly as they had hoped. Moreover, the appearance on the scene of a radical new regime in Constantinople caused alarm in other countries. The Serbs could only see it as a threat to their Pan-Slav ambitions, and a special Serbian guerrilla unit known as četniks was set up to stage raids on Turkish military posts within the neighbouring state of Macedonia. Crete increased its demands for independence and union with Greece, and Britain, to whom the Young Turks turned to try to rescue them from the stifling attentions of their German allies, showed itself very lukewarm towards the new regime: the British were hoping to gain the oil fields of the middle east in any carve-up of the Ottoman Empire, so it was not in their interests to get too friendly with the new regime. The most important reaction from the point of view of the future development of the Balkans, however, was that of Austria-Hungary. A resurgent Ottoman Empire did not fit Vienna's outlook at all, and in 1908

Austria responded to the Young Turks' coup by annexing a whole Ottoman province: Bosnia-Herzegovina. This act was to provide the background for the Balkan crisis of 1914 and the subsequent declaration of war.

Turkey: the Sick Man gets out of bed

The Austrian annexation of Bosnia-Herzegovina

THE AUSTRIANS FEARED that under the new regime, Turkish fortunes in the Balkans might revive and in particular that the Turks might take back into their own hands the administration of Bosnia-Herzegovina, which had been devolved to the Austrians under the terms of the 1878 Treaty of Berlin. To forestall such a move, the Austrian Foreign Minister, Count Aerenthal, hatched a plot to make Austrian administration of the provinces permanent by formally annexing them to the Dual Monarchy. This would have the very pleasing effect of seriously annoying the new regime in Serbia, who could be expected to raise loud protestations, but these could safely be ignored unless the Serbs persuaded the Russians to support them. Aerenthal therefore needed to square the Russians before moving to take over the provinces.

His task was made immeasurably easier by the gullible and frankly rather dim character of his Russian opposite number, Alexander Izvolsky. Aerenthal met Izvolsky and the two men did a deal which involved such a comprehensive breach of international law that Izvolsky dared not reveal it to the Russian prime minister, Piotr Stolypin, for fear that Stolypin would disown it and, in all probability, have him sacked. Izvolsky promised that Russia would make no protest if Austria-Hungary occupied the provinces, and

Aerenthal assured Izvolsky that Austria-Hungary would raise no objection to the Russian fleet sailing through the Dardanelles and out into the Mediterranean. Both undertakings were in breach of the 1878 Treaty of Berlin, but Aerenthal's move did at least have a certain logic to it: Austria-Hungary was already administering the two provinces under the terms of the treaty, and to move from administering an Ottoman province to annexing it outright was something both France and Britain could hardly complain about too loudly since they had done much the same themselves with Ottoman provinces in North Africa. On the other hand, the passage of the Russian fleet through the Dardanelles was strictly forbidden under the terms of the treaty and, as Aerenthal knew full well (and Izvolsky should have known) Britain certainly, and France probably, would take military action to enforce the prohibition. When Aerenthal announced, therefore, that Austria-Hungary was annexing the two provinces, Serbia protested vigorously, as Aerenthal had expected it would, but from the Russian foreign minister came a deafening silence. If Izvolsky spoke up against the Austrian move, Aerenthal could reveal the details of their secret deal, which would infuriate the other Great Powers and seriously damage relations with Serbia, whom Izvolsky was, in effect, selling down the river; the rest of Europe would then go on a war footing to stop the Russians sending their fleet through the Dardanelles. Izvolsky therefore had to remain quietly fuming while Aerenthal announced the annexation and disclaimed all knowledge of any deal respecting the Dardanelles: Izvolsky could hardly protest without betraying his own less-than-honourable role in the affair. The 1908 Austrian annexation of Bosnia-Herzegovina was therefore deeply humiliating for the Russians and hardly less so for the Serbs, who had expected Russian backing against Vienna and hadn't had it. Nor was that the end of the Serbs' frustrations deriving from Austrian policy in Bosnia.

The Austrians wanted Bosnia-Herzegovina for a very specific purpose. The Dual Monarchy was an uneasy compromise struck back in 1867 under which the Austrians and Hungarians effectively shared power. The Austrians, however, had never been fully reconciled to what to them was a loss of the full power over their lands that they had previously enjoyed, and they were always on the lookout for a strong national group which could in some way counter-balance the power of the Hungarians within the Dual Monarchy. The people best placed geographically and politically for the Austrians' purposes were the Serbs of Bosnia–Herzegovina. Once the provinces had been annexed, it was imperative that they should be encouraged to reconcile themselves to their new status within the Dual Monarchy by a conciliatory and accommodating policy towards them. Bosnia–Herzegovina was therefore granted considerable control over its own affairs, with minimal Austrian interference and supervision. The mastermind behind this new policy for keeping the Dual Monarchy together and, ultimately, enhancing the role within it of the Austrians, was the heir to the throne, the Imperial Archduke Franz Ferdinand.

The Austrian annexation of Bosnia-Herzegovina

The Balkan Wars

Serb nationalists after the 'loss' of Bosnia-Herzegovina in 1908 were therefore in an unenviable position. Without Bosnia-Herzegovina, their dream of a Pan-Slav state was impossible, but without Russian help there was nothing they could do about it. What changed the situation was the successful Italian attack on Tripoli and the Dodecanese islands in 1911-12. The revelation that the famed Young Turks might be no more military competent than Abdul Hamid II had been provided the inspiration the Balkan states needed: in 1912 a Balkan League, consisting of Serbia, Greece, Bulgaria and Montenegro, launched a co-ordinated attack that caught the Turks on the back foot. Turkey-in-Europe was reduced in size to the narrow strip of land behind Constantinople, and the victors of what became known as the First Balkan War were therefore able to divide the rest of the former Turkish territory among them.

They were not, however, able to divide it to their collective satisfaction. Bulgaria, still angry at the way it had been treated by the Congress of Berlin in 1878, accused the Greeks of keeping hold of 'Bulgarian' Salonika; the Bulgarians also resented having to hand back Adrianople, which they had taken off the Turks and were hoping to keep. Serbia did well out of the war and might have developed into a formidable regional power had it been able to obtain access to the sea; however the Austrians insisted on the creation of the independent state of Albania specifically in order to deny Serbia access to the coast. 1913 therefore saw a second Balkan War, as Bulgaria turned on its former allies. This second Balkan War brought no joy for Bulgaria, which was heavily defeated, but it gave little to Serbia either; despite being on the wining side, Serbia had still not been able to take hold of a port and would therefore never be able to develop into even a second-rank European Power.[5] The peace settlement was imposed on the Balkan states by the Great Powers acting together in the 1913 Treaty of London; Serbian nationalists, however, reserved their anger at the unsatisfactory outcome entirely for Vienna, which had continually thwarted their Pan-Slav ambitions. There seemed very little the Serbs could do about it: the Serbian prime minister, Nikola Pasic, was a pragmatic politician who, like King Alexander before him, saw the benefits of maintaining good relations with Vienna. What Serbian nationalists needed, therefore, was a way of striking at Austria that Vienna could not ignore and which would provoke a regional war, in which the Russians would be duty-bound to back the Serbs and force a peace settlement on Vienna. At the very least, they thought, Serbia might get a seaport out of it; ideally, it would get the whole of Bosnia-Herzegovina. What better way was there of provoking the right level of anger and indignation in Vienna than by assassinating the heir to the throne?

---

5   Ironically, the one power which did do well from the war was Turkey, which fought off Bulgarian attempts to retake Adrianople and even extended its European territory slightly.

Why the First World War broke out

The Assassination

THE 'BLACK HAND' WAS NOT QUITE AS FEARSOME as its sinister name might suggest. It was a very junior outfit among a large number of clandestine groups set up in Serbia in the aftermath of the 1903 coup. Its 'parent group' was *Narodna Odbrana* ('National Defence'), a secret society set up after the Austro-Hungarian takeover of Bosnia-Herzegovina in 1908 which included high-ranking figures like 'Colonel Apis' and his colleague Major Tankosiz: it was Tankosiz who actually supplied the 1914 conspirators with their weapons and trained them – insofar as they were capable of being trained – in their use. Until 1914 the Black Hand's attempts at assassination had all failed in tragic-comic circumstances and the events of 28 June in Sarajevo started off in the same manner. Franz Ferdinand's presence in Sarajevo that day was itself the result of a bizarre combination of political and personal factors. Although something of a boorish character himself, he was deeply in love with his wife, a Czech Countess called Sophie Chotek. The stiflingly strict rules of etiquette at Franz Josef's court, however, did not allow a mere countess, and a Czech countess to boot, to walk or sit alongside a Prince of the Blood of the imperial House of Habsburg, just because she happened to be married to him. The couple's wedding anniversary was coming up at the end of June and the Archduke was understandably reluctant to undergo yet another round of public occasions at which his wife was obliged to walk a few steps behind him. A possible solution lay in Bosnia-Herzegovina, where, as Inspector-General of the Army rather than as Imperial Prince, the Archduke could spend the day in full ceremonial rig with his wife, as Mrs Inspector-General, sitting beside him. So it was that the Archduke set off for the Bosnian capital, where he and his wife were greeted by the military governor, General Potiorek. From a Serbian nationalist point of view, however, the Archduke's presence in Sarajevo that day was an intolerable provocation. Not only was it a reminder of Austria's occupation of what Serbs regarded as Serbian territory, but 28 June also happened to be the Serbs' national day, the anniversary of their defeat by the Turks in the 1389 Battle of Kosovo, a sort of Serbian Battle of Hastings. The leadership of the Black Hand decided that 28 June was a very good day for Franz Ferdinand, heir to the latest foreign power to occupy Serbian territory, to die.

True to form, the Black Hand made a mess of planning and carrying out their plan. The chosen assassins were not experienced killers but a group of excitable school students, studying for the Bosnian equivalent of their A-levels. The Serbian government got wind of what was afoot and ordered the police to look into what Narodna Odbrana might be up to but did not tip off the Austrians, partly because this might have cast suspicion on exactly how much Belgrade knew about what was afoot, and partly because the Serbian government didn't take the threat from such an apparently incompetent gang as the Black hand entirely seriously. Their view seems to have found an echo in Narodna Odbrana itself: when Apis told its central committee about the plot on 16 June, the committee angrily voted against it, arguing that if it were to succeed it would unleash consequences for which Serbia was not yet prepared: in this the committee proved unusually perceptive. When the day came, the plotters had the centre of Sarajevo staked out ready for the Archduke's arrival, but when his motorcade appeared, the first two assassins got cold feet. The third assassin, Nedeljko Čabrinović, threw a bomb at the Archduke's car but it bounced back off the car's folded-down hood and exploded behind, injuring some of the official escort. Čabrinović promptly swallowed a cyanide capsule and threw himself dramatically into the river. Unfortunately for him, the pill merely made him vomit and the river was only ankle-deep in any case; he was dragged out and had to be protected by the police from being lynched by the angry crowd. It looked as if the day had been yet another Black Hand fiasco. The Archduke was furious and insisted on changing the schedule of the day in order to fit in a visit to the wounded men of his escort in hospital. Anyone who has ever been involved in the tight timings of a royal visit will appreciate how difficult it would have been to make such a major change to the day's schedule at such short notice, and it is hardly surprising that, in amidst the telephone calls to the hospital and the new briefings to the police and the military escort everyone assumed someone else had told the driver, one Leopold Lojka. No-one had, however, and, as is well known, even though the first two cars carried straight on towards the hospital, Lojka turned off the riverside road, blithely following the original route. When Potiorek told him he was going the wrong way, Lojka stopped the car and went into reverse. As could often happen with such cars, this action stalled the engine. Count Harrach, an army officer who had been in the car with the Archduke in the morning (it was in fact his own car), had taken up a defensive position standing on the car's running board on the left hand side; on its unprotected right hand side, however, was Schiller's café, where one of the remaining plotters, the nineteen-year old Gavrilo Princip, was sitting in a panic, wondering what on earth to do. One can only imagine his amazement as, quite out of the blue, an open-topped car carrying the Archduke, the Archduchess and Potiorek, with no protection between him and them, not only drew up right in front of him but conveniently stopped. Not many assassins get a second chance like this and fewer still are presented with such an easy target. He took out his pistol, walked a couple of steps across the pavement and onto the car's right-hand running board, and fired. The first

The Assassination

shot killed the Archduke, the second his wife. Franz Ferdinand had time to urge Sophie to live for the children, but she was already dead. Moments later, so was he. The Black Hand had finally got their first kill.

The July Crisis

Rather like the international reaction to the attacks on New York and Washington on 11 September 2001, the initial response around Europe to the news of the assassination was one of sympathy with the Austrians and fury with the Serbs. Serbia had been regarded with considerable suspicion by the international community ever since the shockingly violent overthrow of King Alexander in 1903: Britain had severed diplomatic relations with Belgrade for three years and, ironically, in the light of later events, the Russians had actually suggested that Austria-Hungary send troops into Serbia to restore order. Pasić was trying hard to restore the country's international reputation but his task was made much harder by Apis and his hardline nationalist followers. By June 1914 the struggle between Pasić and Apis was out in the open. Crown Prince Alexander, a moderate and deeply distrustful of Apis, was taking over as Regent from his father, Apis's protégé King Peter. On 24th June Pasić announced new elections for early July and the campaign pitted him against his arch-rival, Apis. However, the fact that Pasić had clearly been unable to prevent his rival from launching an assassination squad into a neighbouring state with which Pasić claimed to want good relations suggested to the rest of Europe that Serbia was, to all intents and purposes, a genuinely dangerous rogue state.

The Austrian military commander, General Conrad von

Hötzendorf, argued for a tough Austrian military response, marching into Belgrade and imposing draconian terms on the Serb government. Conrad was something of a caricaturist's dream – a moustachioed general whose instinctive response to almost any event was to demand military action: he had been sacked by the Emperor in 1912 at the time of the Italian-Turkish war, for demanding that Austria-Hungary invade northern Italy and take back some of the lands the Austrians had lost there in the nineteenth century. It was Franz Ferdinand who had got him reinstated, so his pugnacious response to his patron's murder is perhaps understandable. Moreover, his point that a retaliatory strike against Belgrade would meet with general international support, or at least acceptance, could well have been right, such was the abhorrence with which the Great powers regarded the Serbian style of politics. That, however, was not an option open to the Austrian Foreign Minister, Count Berchtold. Berchthold and his wife had been good friends of Franz Ferdinand and Sophie, and he seems to have been genuinely upset by their deaths. However, he was far too pragmatic a politician to share General Conrad's outlook: the days when Vienna could simply order troops into another country were long gone. For one thing, such a move would need the emperor's permission and Franz Josef, devastated by yet another assassination in his family, was in no mood to launch another war. Moreover, under the terms of the 1867 Compromise which had set up the Dual Monarchy, a decision for war would need the approval of the Hungarian Parliament too, and the Hungarian prime minister, István Tisza, was equally cautious about launching a strike on Serbia, not, let it be said, from humanitarian considerations but because he thought a successful war which brought even more Serbs within the Dual Monarchy would be bound to work to Hungary's disadvantage. Moreover, Tsiza was far more concerned than Conrad about the likely reaction of the Russians. Given the wrangling between these key figures, therefore, it was not until Saturday 4 July, nearly a week after the assassination, that Berchtold sent an envoy, Count von Hoyos, to Berlin to sound out the German government on what their reaction would be to tough Austrian action in the Balkans. Hoyos found himself dealing directly with the Kaiser; the German Foreign Minister was on honeymoon and the Kaiser ran his reply only briefly past the German Chancellor, Theodore Bethmann Hollweg. The Kaiser's reply, delivered to the Austrian ambassador in Berlin, was that Germany would stand by Austria-Hungary according to the terms both of their alliance and of the two monarchs' 'ancient friendship'. This suggested that Germany would support Austria-Hungary over and above the conditions of their alliance – in other words, Germany would stand behind the Austrians *no matter what they might choose to do*. For this reason, this German assurance of support is known to historians as the 'blank cheque'. It doesn't necessarily follow from this that either the Kaiser or Bethmann Hollweg were expecting that war would definitely follow; the blank cheque meant that any Austro-Hungarian ambassador or envoy could tell the Serbs or the Russians, with full authority, that everything Austria-Hungary was doing was being done with German support and approval. In that way, the blank cheque could be seen as a way of warning the Russians off and *averting* a general European war. However, it did not work out that way and the German government did not really want it to, either.

Any crisis quickly develops its own momentum: in the case of the 1914 one, this was, at first, very slow. The Austrian reaction was stretched out by ponderous and agonising discussion for almost a month. The 'blank cheque' was issued on Sunday 5 July, a week to the day after the assassination; the government of Austria-Hungary only finally decided on its response to the assassination two weeks later, on Sunday 19 July, a full three weeks after the shooting, and it did not deliver it to the Serbian government until the following Friday, 24 July, almost a month after the event. In that time the initial sense of outrage had faded and the international news agenda had moved on to other things: the tough Austrian demands of the Serbs now appeared vindictive, calculating and self-interested.

The July Crisis

The delay in the Austrian response was caused by a number of factors, mainly concerned with obtaining support from all sectors of the Dual Monarchy for a tough line to be taken with the Serbs, but also influenced, at least in the timing of the ultimatum itself, by the chance factor that the French President, Poincaré, and the prime minister, Viviani, were at sea, on their way home from a state visit to Russia, and would therefore be unable to respond as quickly as the crisis would demand. For the Austrians had decided to use Germany's promise of unquestioning support to put the screws on Serbia once and for all: on 24 July they presented the Serbian government with an ultimatum, demanding that it hand over the investigations into the assassination and into the Black Hand to the Austro-Hungarian authorities, even allowing Austrian police to operate within Serbia. The Serbs had forty eight hours in which to reply. The terms were so harsh that, if they had accepted them fully the Serbs would in effect be surrendering their sovereignty and accepting Austria-Hungary's authority over their internal affairs. The Austrians clearly didn't expect the Serbs to accept the terms and the Austrian minister in Belgrade had his bags packed ready for an immediate departure as soon as the Serbs handed him their reply. When it arrived on 25 July, however, the reply was not at all the defiant or indignant document the Austrians had expected: Pasić had assured himself of Russian support, but he did not want to provoke a war. Pasić's reply accepted all the Austrian demands except that for Austrian police to operate within Serbia, and he was not implacably opposed even to that: he merely proposed that it should be put to an international conference for a final decision. By any normal standards, and in any other circumstances, the Serbian reply would have been regarded as a major Austrian victory, handing them all they wanted without the need for war; however, the Austrian minister, scanning it and seeing that one of the terms was not explicitly granted, declared that the reply was not good enough, picked up his passport and headed for the railway station.

Berlin's role

VIENNA COULD NOT IMMEDIATELY DECLARE WAR on Serbia, however, because there were worrying signs of back-pedalling from Berlin, where the Kaiser seemed to be responding positively to a series of initiatives coming out of London for a negotiated settlement of the crisis. The British government was heavily taken up in August 1914 with the threat of full-scale civil war in Ireland and British political and public opinion only caught up belatedly with the growing crisis in the Balkans. The British Foreign Secretary, Sir Edward Grey, suggested extending the time limit on the Austrian ultimatum to Serbia and followed this up with a proposal that Austria-Hungary and Serbia might accept mediation by the Great Powers. The Kaiser seemed inclined to accept the British proposals; however Bethmann Hollweg and the German Foreign Minister, Gottlieb von Jagow, now returned from honeymoon, systematically scuppered all British peace initiatives. On 25 July, for example, when he received Grey's plea that Serbia be given more time, Jagow deliberately delayed sending it on to Vienna until he was sure it would arrive too late to stop the ultimatum's being sent. On Monday 27 July Jagow saw the Serbian reply to the Austrian ultimatum; knowing that the Kaiser would seize on it as an opportunity to avoid war (as indeed he did), Jagow did not show it to him until the following morning, by which time events had moved on. Also on the Monday, Grey proposed that Britain and Germany acting together might be able to restrain the Austrians and prevent the crisis from erupting into war. Bethmann Hollweg kept the proposal from the Kaiser, sent it to Vienna with a covering note advising Berchtold to reject it, and told the German ambassador in London to decline it. The next day, 28 July, when it was clear that Austria-Hungary was about to declare war on Serbia, the Kaiser drew up a proposal by which the Austrians would take Belgrade and then stop, allowing the Serbs to negotiate a deal they could honourably accept; the Austrians could then go home. This 'Halt in Belgrade' proposal would have given Austria-Hungary an equivalent of Prussia's victory in the Franco-Prussian War: defeat and humiliation for the Serbs but not outright annexation of their whole country. This proposal too fell victim to intervention by Bethmann Hollweg, who first delayed the telegram to Vienna that contained it and then so altered it as to obscure the Kaiser's actual proposal.

In the light of what we know was about to happen, it is fair to ask what on earth Bethmann Hollweg and Jagow thought they were playing at. They had, between them, removed all the brakes that were being applied to Austria-Hungary's drive for war, including those applied by their own Kaiser. Does this mean that the blame for the First World War can be placed on their shoulders? Those who hold Germany responsible for the outbreak of war can certainly ask some very serious questions of both men's conduct in these crucial days at the end of July. Bethmann was an unashamed German nationalist and expansionist: he had ambitions for German expansion within Europe as well as in Germany's overseas colonies. He was nervous of the growing power of Russia and he shared the widely-held view that Germany was better advised to seek an early showdown with the Russians rather than waiting until Russia's military reforms rendered her too strong to beat. None of this necessarily explains his conduct in July 1914 however. To put his actions in perspective, consider for a moment the alternative he was facing. Serbia was engaged in what would nowadays be called the state sponsorship of terrorism. If Sir Edward Grey were to get his international conference, whether it were to be a meeting of heads of government or merely a conference of ambassadors, it would listen to both sides of the argument and then it would broker a settlement. Unless there were decisive proof that the Serbian government had actually ordered the assassination, which seemed unlikely, it was inconceivable that such a settlement would actually eliminate Serbia as an independent state. In other words, the Serbs would, quite literally, have got away with murder. The Austrians, on the other hand, would have shown the world that any state could send assassins to kill any member of its government or imperial family, including the heir to the throne himself, and still Vienna would take no action. In such a volatile multi-ethnic empire, such a message was potentially disastrous: what if other national groups decided to launch their own hit squads? Germany's main ally could be in danger of imploding unless it showed its muscle, and that could only be done by taking firm decisive military action. German support would guard against the danger of Russian intervention, and a short, decisive war, along the Clausewitzian lines that had served Prussia so well a generation ago, could guarantee Austria-Hungary's survival well into the foreseeable future. Failure to take such action could have untold consequences.

So, when Austria-Hungary finally declared war on Serbia on Tuesday 28 July, a month to the day after the Sarajevo assassination, three weeks after the German 'blank cheque' and three days after the 'unacceptable' Serbian response to the Austrian ultimatum, it was turning its back quite deliberately on British attempts to provide a negotiated settlement and placing its trust entirely in Germany's assurances of whole-hearted diplomatic and military support. It immediately became clear that that support would almost certainly be needed. The following day, as Austrian troops started shelling Belgrade and the German ambassador in St Petersburg warned the Russian government not to start mobilising its troops, Berlin sent the text of an ultimatum to its ambassador in Brussels, to be kept ready for delivery to the Belgian government: already the machinery of the Schlieffen Plan was cranking into operation.

Berlin's role

Russia acts

AFTER A LONG PERIOD in which little seemed to be happening, events now started happening with such bewildering speed that it is difficult to discern that anyone was actually in control of them. Until Wednesday 29 July, the war was still an entirely Austro-Serb affair; however, on that day Tsar Nicholas II ordered the mobilisation of Russia's vast military resources against Austria-Hungary and on Thursday 30, advised by his generals that it was impracticable to mobilise against only one country, he gave the order for general mobilisation, along the German border as well. That one decision transformed the 'Third Balkan War' into a European war. Why did Nicholas do it?

As with so many of the decisions of 1914, the Russian decision to mobilise is best understood not in terms of what they hoped to achieve but in terms of what they feared would happen if they didn't. Without Russian help, Serbia would unquestionably fall to the Austrians. While an international conference would probably have retained an independent Serbia, there was no knowing what a victorious Austria-Hungary might do if its armies marched triumphantly into a besieged and battered Belgrade. It was entirely possible that Austria-Hungary might absorb all or most of Serbia into its own borders, just as it had done with Bosnia-Herzegovina; and indeed we know that there were powerful voices in the Austro-Hungarian government arguing just that. The destruction of

Serbia, especially coming so soon after Russia's failure to stand by the Serbs in 1908, would almost certainly signal the end of Russia's hopes of a decisive voice in the future of the Balkans. Austria-Hungary would now be the dominant power in the region, and 1914 would be yet another date in the long list of Russia's Balkan failures, alongside the Crimean War, the Congress of Berlin and the 'loss' of Bosnia-Herzegovina. But if Russia were intending to move it would need to do so fast: even the Austro-Hungarian army ought to be able to make short work of overrunning Serbia. The obvious worry for the Russians was that mobilising their forces would provoke a strong German response, and indeed on 30 July the German ambassador in St Petersburg, Count Friedrich Pourtalès, warned the Tsar that Germany would mobilise its own forces unless the Russians immediately cancelled their own mobilisation plans. The Russians might plausibly hope to give the Austrians a run for their money, but they could not regard war with Germany quite so complacently. The reason they did not back down in the face of German warnings is largely down to the encouragement they received from France's fire-eating ambassador in St Petersburg, Maurice Paléologue, who went far beyond the actual terms of French government policy in promising French support if Russia were to stand up to the Germans. Paléologue also misled ministers in Paris as to the true state of Russian mobilisation, so that Paris thought it was supporting *partial* Russian mobilisation, against Austria-Hungary only, whereas Russia had already moved beyond that to *general* mobilisation, against Germany as well. At 4.00 pm on Thursday 30 July Nicholas II gave orders for the general mobilisation of the Russian army.

What were the chances that Russian mobilisation would actually deter the Germans? On the face of it, they seem to have been slim: Jagow was not deterred and von Moltke, the Chief of the German General Staff, was urging the Austrians to mobilise their forces against Russia as well as the Serbs. However, 30 July was also the day on which Bethmann Hollweg seems to have developed cold feet, recommending that Austria-Hungary open talks with Russia and look much more seriously at the British proposals for mediation. Bethmann's remained a solitary voice (and the Austrians were in any case receiving completely contradictory messages from von Moltke, the military chief), and he soon recovered his nerve. But what if Russia were to hold back from mobilisation? That would pull the rug from under the feet of the hawks in Berlin. The Russians would certainly not be inclined to restrain themselves, given how much prestige was at stake, but they might find themselves constrained to do so if the French withheld their support. What was Paris' role in the crisis?

Russia acts

France's role

THE ONLY POWER which could hope to exercise direct influence on Russia's course of action was France, its only ally. The original 1894 Franco-Russian alliance had been aimed against Britain, whose colonial interests appeared to threaten both countries, but since then the political landscape had changed fundamentally: fears of Britain abroad had been replaced by the much more immediate fear of Germany at home. Unlike the 1904 Anglo-French entente, which allowed for military 'conversations' and collaboration between the two countries, the 1907 Anglo-Russian entente had no such military dimension: Russia's only hope for international support was its alliance with France.

Like all such agreements, the Franco-Russian alliance was very precise in its terms. Firstly, the two powers agreed to consult with each other before embarking on war: by chance, this could be done more directly than usual in 1914 because of Poincaré and Viviani's presence in St Petersburg just as the crisis got under way. Secondly, if any of the Triple Alliance Powers (i.e. Germany, Austria-Hungary and Italy; Turkey was not a member of the Triple Alliance) were to mobilise its forces, France and Russia would mobilise in response. As of Poincaré's return to France on Wednesday 29 July, the only one of the Triple Alliance Powers to have mobilised was Austria-Hungary, and that had only been against Serbia: there was no need, therefore, for this provision to be enacted. Thirdly, if either

France or Russia were *attacked* by Germany, each would come to the other's aid. Again, this was not happening by the time of Poincaré's return. In theory, therefore, France was free to negotiate, restrain the Russians or do anything necessary to safeguard peace until such time as Germany mobilised (when France was duty-bound to mobilise too) or launched an attack on Russia (when France was obliged to go to Russia's support). Unfortunately, a remarkable train of coincidences, bad luck and bad timing, had the cumulative effect of completely blunting France's ability to do anything at all to prevent events from moving towards war.

Although most French statesmen shared the country's popular anti-German sentiment, there was one important exception. Joseph Caillaux was a hard-nosed Radical with an almost Thatcher-like relish for undertaking policies that were bound to be massively unpopular: as Finance Minister from 1913 Caillaux was heavily engaged in introducing a British-style income tax, a project that attracted enormous public odium and fury. The anger was all the greater because Caillaux was already deeply distrusted because of his proven readiness to reach diplomatic accord with Germany. As prime minister at the time of the 1911 Agadir crisis he had struck what was in fact a highly advantageous deal with the Germans, but he had done it by negotiating behind the back of his own Foreign Ministry and the angry public backlash at was deemed his treacherous behaviour had forced him to resign. He was far too powerful a political force to be kept out of office for long, however, and he was brought back into office as finance minister in 1913. As the Austro-Serbian crisis unfolded and threatened to involve both Russia and Germany, Poincaré knew that Caillaux would be putting his considerable political weight into the scales in favour of restraining the Russians and reaching a mutually satisfactory accommodation with Berlin. And so, indeed, he might have done, had not fate, in the form of his wife, delivered Caillaux a quite extraordinary blow. In its campaign against Caillaux's income tax proposals, the Parisian daily *Le Figaro* had embarked on a series of

attacks of remarkable viciousness on Caillaux's record and person-
ality; it amounted indeed to a smear campaign and was suspected,
rightly, of being conducted by his political rivals. When it appeared
that the attacks were about to start exploring his not-unspotted
personal life, Madame Caillaux took matters into her own hand.
Like a latter-day Charlotte Corday, and entirely without her hus-
band's knowledge, she bought herself a pistol, went to the offices of
the *Le Figaro*, and shot the editor dead. Not surprisingly, France was
immediately gripped by the details of what by any standards was a
sensational story of politics, love and murder, and Madame Caillaux' trial, which did not in any way disappoint those hoping for
high courtroom drama, dominated the French press and completely took up public and political attention (many of Caillaux's opponents had reason to fear what revelations might emerge in court)
over the crucial days in July when the rest of Europe was watching
events unfolding in the Balkans. Perhaps even more momentously,
Caillaux felt obliged to resign from the government. The one man
with the political stature to turn France from its blindly pro-Rus-
sian course was removed from the political scene just at the point
when he could have made most of a difference.

Poincaré and Viviani's presence in St Petersburg also proved, in
the event, a piece of very unlucky timing. They were in Russia at
the point when the Austrians sent their ultimatum to Serbia but
before it was known what would follow. There was not much either man could say to their Russian hosts at that stage other than
to encourage them to offer support to the Serbs without taking
things too far. They set sail for France just before the text of the
Serbian reply became known and were effectively incommunica-
do at sea during all the frantic diplomatic moves that followed on
from the Serbian reply, Grey's compromise proposals, Russia's decision for partial mobilisation and the Austrian declaration of war
on Serbia. During the crucial stage, therefore, when it might have
been possible to persuade the Russians to pursue a more conciliatory line, French foreign policy was in the hands of inexperienced

stand-ins in Paris (Viviani was foreign minister as well as premier), who promptly started to reassure Russia of French support far beyond the actual terms of the 1894 alliance.

Even had they wished to give the Russians a different message, these stand-in ministers would have found their task made much harder by the actions of two men, Paléologue, the French Ambassador in St Petersburg, and the French military commander-in-chief, General Joffre. Paléologue was now routinely exceeding his brief by assuring the Russians of French diplomatic and military support while also concealing from Paris the full extent of Russian military preparations. Bienvenu-Martin, the stand-in foreign minister during Viviani's absence, and Messimy, the war minister, thought Russia was only ordering partial mobilisation, against Austria-Hungary, and could therefore safely be encouraged from Paris, when in fact preparations were at an advanced stage for general mobilisation, against Germany as well. Meanwhile, Joffre was not only lobbying French ministers for immediate mobilisation if France were not be placed at a catastrophic disadvantage when war finally broke out, but on 25 July, while Poincaré and Viviani were still in Russia, on no authority whatsoever he assured the Russian ambassador that France would support Russia in any war that might break out and reminded him that Russia was itself committed to a military strike into East Prussia. By the time Poincaré and Viviani got back to Paris on 29 July, much of the damage had been done: the Russians had been led by French assurances to decide in favour of a General Mobilisation regardless of the German response. Had either man been strongly opposed to war with Germany they could still have imposed their authority on their subordinates and altered France's course, but they weren't and they didn't. On the day he got back Poincaré invited Sir Francis Bertie and Alexander Izvolsky, the British and Russian ambassadors, to the Elysée Palace, where it was decided that if Russia were to issue orders for a General Mobilisation, France would support her. Poincaré had now committed France to full support of the Russians beyond the terms of the alliance, and had thereby denied France any chance of negotiating any sort of peaceful or compromise settlement.

Only one major question remained for the French before they could safely commit themselves to war: would the country unite behind the flag or would it split? A country which had gone through the carnage of the suppression of the Commune and the bitter recriminations of the Dreyfus Case could not take its national unity for granted. Here too fate or chance or unlucky timing played a remarkably dramatic part that eventful Parisian summer. Apart from Caillaux, the most influential anti-war voice in French politics was that of the socialist leader Jean Jaurès. Socialist movements were beginning to mobilise themselves in an attempt to halt what by the last days of July seemed an unstoppable slide towards war; however, as soon as the German government started to make its own war preparations known, its country's socialists, with very few exceptions, put their principles on one side and rallied to their national flag. Of all Europe's socialist leaders, Jaurès was therefore both the best placed and the most inclined to put the case against war and to drive a wedge between the different groups in French politics and society. He was unable to do so, however, because on Friday 31 July, as he sat with friends in his usual Paris café, he was assassinated. The assassin was a self-absorbed ultra-nationalist unemployed schoolteacher but, as usually happens with political assassinations, the conspiracy theories began immediately. The word on the boulevards was that 'They' had killed Jaurès, 'they' being either the French Right (which had indeed talked in the press of shooting him) or the Russian secret services. The government's fear now was of a socialist rising that would paralyse any military move France might seek to make in support of the Russians; Poincaré therefore kept a close and nervous eye on all reports of reactions in socialist circles to the assassination. But, against all expectations, the socialist press urged its readers to avenge Jaurès by a show of national unity behind the government and against France's enemies. Poincaré could breathe again while Jaurès could start turning in his newly-dug grave.

France's role

The Failure of Containment

THE BRITISH WERE STILL HOLDING OUT for an international congress to resolve the crisis before it got out of hand; Grey backed up his proposal by warning the German ambassador to London that Britain might yet be drawn into the war if the Germans were to attack France. With the Austro-Serbian war now started, Grey's offer was potentially more attractive to the Germans than it had been earlier. If Austria were to come to an international congress with its troops in possession of Belgrade and of all or most of Serbia, Vienna would be in a much stronger position than it would have been before hostilities commenced. Bethmann Hollweg, perhaps also having second thoughts about where the crisis might be heading, therefore passed the British offer on to Vienna with a note of caution not to reject it out of hand; Count Berchtold, however, delayed reading the British proposal until the afternoon, by which time the news of Russia's mobilisation had rendered talk of an international congress redundant. In any case, von Moltke, the Head of the German General Staff, was giving Berchtold completely different advice, urging him to mobilise fully in answer to the Russian move. Confident of German support, Berchtold took von Moltke's advice: at 12.30 pm on Friday 31 July Austria-Hungary mobilised its armed forces.

On the last day of July, therefore, it seemed inevitable that the Austro-Serbian war would spread to Russia, in which case a second front would presumably open up along the extensive Austro-Russian border. This was a much bigger undertaking than the Austrian government had envisaged when it sent its ultimatum to Serbia only a week earlier. Equally predictably, at 7.00 pm that same evening, 31 July, Germany declared itself in 'danger of war', a sort of "alert state red", and it began to mobilise its troops the following day. The Serbian crisis had now created a war across southern and eastern Europe, from Belgrade to the Baltic. Could it possibly be prevented from extending to the west? This question became the focus of British, French and even German efforts over the next twenty four hours.

Britain's proposals

ON FRIDAY 31 JULY, as the situation in Austria and Russia reached crisis point, Sir Edward Grey spoke with the German ambassador in London, Prince Lichnowsky. He made it clear that if the French and Russians rejected reasonable offers from Germany, then Britain would stand back and leave them to sort out their own differences with Germany. However, if Germany were to make unreasonable demands of France, or invade with no pretext at all, then Britain would stand by the French. As Lichnowsky almost certainly realised, Grey was on tricky ground here. The Cabinet, which had been discussing the crisis for the past two days, was by no means united in supporting the French. The feeling in London was that events were spiralling out of control and that it was time for someone to apply a strong restraining hand: Britain and Germany might conceivably be able to apply such a hand to Austria-Hungary, but only France could restrain the Russians. Lichnowsky was no warmonger and he shared the Kaiser's enthusiasm for England and all things English. The version of his conversation with Grey which he sent to Berlin, where it arrived by telegram on Saturday 1 August, went significantly further than Grey had said. Lichnowsky reported that Britain would keep France neutral under British guarantee: only if the Germans attacked her would Britain declare war on Germany. The telegram arrived just as German mobilisation was being put into operation and it encouraged the Kaiser to demand that troop movements towards the west be halted immediately, ignoring von Moltke's tearful protests that such an alteration to Schlieffen's great Plan was tantamount to blasphemy and could not, in any case, be done.

This German dependence on Britain's response might seem surprising, especially given the small size of Britain's army; the Kaiser himself would shortly be referring to it as a 'contemptible' little army. Yet the Germans generally held the British in very high regard and they were acutely aware of the enormous resources Britain had at its disposal. The British Expeditionary Force might be small, but then Britain did not have conscription: it could soon put much larger armies into the field (as indeed happened). Moreover, both Britain's fleet and its enormous overseas empire gave Britain huge potential to harm Germany both at home and abroad. Above all, unlike France or Russia, Britain had no obvious grudge against Germany beyond exasperation, shared by many in the German government and military, at the antics and tactlessness of the Kaiser. The Germans therefore seized on any evidence that came their way that Britain might stay out of the war and, even better, might keep one or other of its entente partners out of the war too. On 26 July, for example, when the Serbian reply to the Austrian ultimatum was still the news story of the day, Prince Henry of Prussia, the Kaiser's younger brother, met their cousin, King George V. George said that Britain would try to stay out of any war that might yet develop; when he got back to Germany, Prince Henry reported this to the Kaiser as a solemn declaration from the British monarch that Britain would stay neutral, a totally different thing. The Kaiser took 'the word of a King' entirely to heart and was then outraged by any suggestion that Britain might, or even could, pursue any other course. Lichnowsky's message was therefore music to Wilhelm's ears: Britain would not only stay neutral, but would keep France neutral too. The whole nightmare prospect of a two-front war seemed to be dissolving in front of Wilhelm's eyes: his disappointment when the dreadful truth dawned that Britain might not stay neutral after all was therefore all the sharper, and helps explain why he convinced himself that the English were the real guilty party in 1914.

By Saturday 1 August, the idea that Britain might save Europe from a war on two fronts existed only in a few fevered imaginations in Berlin; elsewhere the grim reality of a European war was steadily taking shape. The German ambassador in St Petersburg handed Germany's declaration of war to the Russian foreign minister and France issued orders for a general mobilisation of its armed forces. The British still hoped to stay neutral: Winston Churchill gave orders for the mobilisation of the fleet, ostensibly as a defensive precaution, while Grey met the French ambassador, Paul Cambon, and told him that France must make its own mind up; Britain would not be joining in the war as things stood.[6] Cambon was angry and reminded Grey that under the terms of the 1912 naval agreement France had transferred all its naval forces to the Mediterranean, handing over responsibility for defending its Channel and Atlantic coastline to the Royal Navy: what if the German fleet were to appear off Calais or Cherbourg and open fire? Thanks to Britain, the coast would be undefended. Grey saw the force of Cambon's argument and replied that Britain would still undertake to defend the French coast, even if it remained neutral in the war. This was cloudcuckooland thinking: a neutral country may defend its own coastline by all the means in its power, but it cannot undertake to defend the coastline of one belligerent against attacks by another without casting away its own neutrality. By undertaking to defend the French coastline, Grey was throwing away any hope of maintaining British neutrality at the very moment when he was asserting it.

The final nail in the coffin of the illusion of British neutrality came in the form of a telegram from George V to the Kaiser which arrived in Berlin late at night on 1 August. George explained

---

6   Paul Cambon, the French ambassador in London, should not be confused with his brother, Jules Cambon, the French ambassador in Berlin.

Britain's proposals

that Lichnowsky appeared to have misunderstood Britain's position: Britain would guarantee French neutrality *only* if Germany maintained neutrality both towards France *and* towards Russia. If Germany insisted on attacking either of them, then they would each defend themselves and Britain would not stand in their way. The Kaiser flew into a rage at what he saw as British duplicity and dropped all his objections to German war preparation in the west. As Sunday 2 August dawned, German troops crossed into Luxembourg.

A week earlier, all the attention had been on Serbia's reply to the Austrian ultimatum; now all eyes were on western Europe where Paul Cambon, not unreasonably, requested clarification of Sir Edward Grey's offer of British protection of the French Channel coastline. What would Britain do in the event of a German naval assault? Would British ships open fire on the Germans? On Sunday 2 August Grey put the question before the Cabinet. He argued for military action to defend the French, including firing on German vessels, and he was supported by Churchill, the Lord Chancellor Richard Haldane, who had himself tried unsuccessfully to negotiate a peace deal with the Germans two years earlier, and, crucially, the Prime Minister, Herbert Asquith. However others in the Cabinet, led by the veteran Liberal John Morley and the Chancellor of the Exchequer, David Lloyd George, were opposed to the move, pointing out that it would render Britain's neutral stance null and void. Grey won Cabinet backing, but it was clear that ministers were deeply split and those opposed to military action were deeply unhappy at the prospect of its being launched. Then, at 7.00 pm arrived news that Germany had issued an ultimatum to the government of Belgium, demanding passage for its troops through Belgian territory. The Belgian government had refused permission and, with a heavy heart, Asquith ordered the mobilisation of Britain's armed forces.

The following day, Monday 3 August, was a Bank Holiday in Britain and provided a strange lull before the storm that would be unleashed on the Tuesday. Morley and two other opponents of military action resigned from the Cabinet, but not Lloyd George, who had changed his stance in the light of the German threat to Belgium. In the afternoon the House of Commons met and Sir Edward Grey made a long statement laying the situation before MPs, stressing that Britain was under no binding obligation to any other Power but pointing out that under the terms of the 1912 agreement Britain was morally obliged to maintain its guarantee of the French coastline and reminding the House of Britain's treaty commitment, dating back to 1839, to defend the independence and integrity of Belgium. He even pointed out that, apart from the Austrian war with Serbia and the German declaration of war on Russia, it was not entirely clear who had declared war on whom (although during that day Germany did formally declare war on France). Most of the House backed Grey's stand, but the Labour leader Ramsay MacDonald opposed it, arguing that neither Britain's security nor its honour were at stake in a potential German attack upon France. The following day, however, Asquith announced to the House of Commons that German troops had invaded Belgium and that the Belgian king had appealed to Britain for diplomatic support. At 7.00 pm Sir Edward Goschen, the British ambassador in Berlin, handed Bethmann Hollweg a British ultimatum, demanding that Germany withdraw its troops from Belgium, or Britain would declare war. A reply was requested by midnight (11.00 pm London time). No reply was received, and a formal declaration of war was delivered to Lichnowsky by Foreign Office messenger. In a moment of gruesome comedy, it was realised that Lichnowsky had been sent the wrong envelope: he had received the version drawn up in response to a hypothetical German declaration of war on Britain. Harold Nicolson, then a young attaché at the Foreign Office, was sent to the German embassy to summon Lichnowsky from his bed and ask if he could substitute the proper message for the one sent in error. Lichnowsky, looking shattered from the failure of his efforts to avoid war, indicated towards the table where it lay

Britain's proposals

apparently unread. Nicolson exchanged it for the 'real' declaration, got Lichnowsky to sign a receipt and took his leave. Lichnowsky's last words to him were to pass on his best regards to Nicolson's father.

The round of declarations of war was not quite over: two days after the British declaration of war, Austria-Hungary finally declared war on Russia, while Serbia, facing the inevitable, declared war on Germany. Military campaigning had already begun, as German troops poured into Belgium and northern France and French troops gathered for an invasion across the German border. In Britain, excited crowds piled into recruiting offices as soon as the declaration of war was known. Sir Edward Grey's famous comment, as he watched the lamplighters at work in Whitehall, that the lamps were being extinguished all over Europe and he would not see them relit in his lifetime, was a lyrical testament to the comprehensive failure of the efforts of statesmen and diplomats all over the continent to perform what is usually the most basic diplomatic task: to avoid going to war. Why did they get things so catastrophically wrong?

Who Was to Blame?

THE BLAME GAME GOT UNDER WAY almost as soon as the war did. It is no great surprise to find opponents in any war blaming each other for starting it, but the atrocities committed by the Germans in Belgium, where German troops set about wholesale executions of the civilian population, served to reassure anyone in Britain who might have found the 1839 Treaty of London, which guaranteed Belgian independence, an inadequate basis for war. Wartime propaganda on both sides routinely portrayed the other as bullying, aggressive and untrustworthy, though the Germans' actual conduct certainly made their enemies' task much easier: Germany was the first belligerent to use poison gas and to launch unrestricted submarine warfare against merchant and passenger vessels, including those belonging to neutral countries. Allied propaganda was therefore able to present the conflict as a war not just to limit German expansion but to safeguard democracy and even civilisation itself: a celebrated American cartoon showed Germany as a great bloodthirsty ape, clutching a bloodied club and wearing a *pickelhaube* helmet inscribed with the word 'militarism'. The appalling nature of the war also added urgency to the search for a culprit. France had lost a quarter of its young male population and suffered extensive destruction of its main industrial region and some of its prime agricultural land; the British had been appalled at the rate of loss of their own volunteers: as the peacemakers gathered in Paris in 1919 it seemed inconceivable to them that a war of such devastation should not have had a very good cause, that it should all have been fought for nothing.

The 'War Guilt Clause'

AT THE PARIS PEACE CONFERENCE, the allies took a decision which was to have lasting consequences. Highly unusually, they inserted a clause into the Treaty of Versailles that specifically stated that Germany accepted responsibility for causing the war and agreed to pay crippling war reparations to cover the reconstruction of towns and countryside ruined in the fighting. Nothing angered the German people more than the humiliation of being made to pay for a war which they did not really accept they had lost in any case, and which they certainly did not believe they had been responsible for starting. This resentment scuppered all attempts by postwar German governments to reach a settlement of the reparations issue and was a significant factor in creating the context and atmosphere for the rise of the Nazis. Why did the allies feel it was necessary to include the 'War Guilt' clause?

As Margaret Macmillan points out in her study of the 1919 peace process, the 'war guilt' clause did not in fact lay the blame for the war solely on Germany: it was simply a necessary legal basis for claiming reparations; there were similar clauses, inserted for the same reason, in the treaties with Germany's allies.[7] Nevertheless, the German clause was the one that caused the trouble. The clause

---

7   Margaret Macmillan, *Peacemaking: six months that changed the world* (London: John Murray, 2002)

was framed at the insistence of the French and British, and it is not difficult to see why they should have insisted on it. In both countries there were urgent public demands for retribution for the deaths and destruction wrought by the war – the call in Britain was to 'hang the Kaiser' – which their governments could hardly ignore. The Americans too were very conscious that they had suffered heavy battlefield losses fighting a form of aggressive militarism which was most evident in the government and society of Imperial Germany. The Germans, on the other hand, took the War Guilt clause to mean they were being held solely responsible for a war in which, they firmly believed, all the governments of Europe had been equally guilty.

The Fischer Thesis

As PASSIONS CALMED DOWN in the decade that followed the peace
treaties, attitudes in the United States and Britain towards German
war guilt began to change. Lloyd George, who had declared in
1919 that his aim was to 'squeeze Germany till the pips squeak',
reflected in his *War Memoirs* that the outbreak of the war had not
been down to one state after all, but rather to a sort of general
drift which had affected all the combatant countries. By the 1920s,
with the Germans openly challenging the validity of the Treaty of
Versailles and demanding its renegotiation, the historical question
of the causation of the war took on an urgent political importance. The inter-war years saw the publication in all the countries
involved of substantial collections of diplomatic correspondence
to 'prove' where the guilt for the war truly lay. These documents
constitute one of the most extensive published collections of archival material for any historical topic in the pre-internet age: they lie
at the root of the various theories about how the war started and
they arm those who refute them. They have been used to blame
the Germans, the British, the Austrians and the Serbs, and also to
support the claim that the war was a general tragedy for which the
diplomatic system and the pre-war society as a whole was to blame.

One of the most comprehensive such collections was put together by the Italian journalist Luigi Albertini. His conclusion was
that, while the Austrians certainly had some very serious explaining

to do about their conduct in 1914, and the other Great Powers could not escape their own share of the responsibility, the main finger of blame had to point to the Germans.[8] This was perhaps an unsurprising conclusion for him to reach, since he was himself an anti-fascist and he was producing his work just as the Germans plunged the world into a second World War. The idea that the War Guilt clause got it about right and that both wars could be ascribed to the Germans remained a popular one during and after the 1939-1945 war: some British writers of the period even referred to 'the First and Second German Wars'.

However, attitudes at least in the English-speaking countries began to change in the 1960s as the Vietnam War forced a reconsideration of whether the causes of wars really justify the death and suffering that warfare inevitably entails. The First World War, whose memory was rekindled by a series of fiftieth anniversary events through the decade, appeared to some as an earlier and even more ghastly version of Vietnam: a brutal war involving untold suffering and destruction for no readily apparent purpose. It was in the 1960s that the poems of the British war poets began to reach a wide audience: the most comprehensive collection of Wilfred Owen's work, for example, *The Collected Poems of Wilfred Owen* was edited by Cecil Day Lewis in 1963 and Benjamin Britten's *War Requiem*, which includes some of Owen's verse, was written in 1962. 1969 saw the reprinting of American writer Dalton Trumbo's anti-war novel *Johnny Got His Gun* about a young American soldier horrifically injured in the First World War; it was followed a couple of years later by a film version. The niceties of pre-1914 European diplomacy often seemed petty and cruelly irrelevant to the sufferings of the soldiers who actually fought in the war that the diplomats declared so blithely from their comfortable offices. The closing sequence of Richard Attenborough's 1969 film of *Oh! What a Lovely War* shows newly killed British soldiers passing from the gritty reality of the

---

8   Luigi Albertini, *The Origins of the War of 1914* tr. Isabella Massey (3vv, London: Enigma, 2005).

trenches into a surreal dreamland, where they see Europe's monarchs and statesmen, immaculately dressed, sitting in an echoing, pristine-white palace, courteously handing round the peace treaty that will end the war that has claimed the watching men's lives: it is a meeting of two completely alien worlds. Academic historians often reinforced the image of the Great War as senseless, unnecessary slaughter: the popular British historian AJP Taylor, for example, put forward the theory that the Powers were victims not just of their own greed and folly but even of their own railway systems, whose timetables were so rigid that once a Power had mobilised it found itself locked into a drive to war which not even tsars or kaisers could reverse.[9]

An intriguingly different interpretation was produced at the beginning of the decade by a German historian, Professor Fritz Fischer of the University of Hamburg. In his book in his book *Griff Nach der Weltmacht* (literally, 'Grab for World Power' but translated into English by the less colourful title, 'Germany's Aims in the First World War'), he produced documentary evidence to suggest that Germany planned during the war to extend its frontiers in both the west and the east.[10] He relied heavily on a document drawn up in September 1914 by Kurt Riezler, Bethmann Hollweg's secretary, which laid out a series of possible war aims for Germany, including annexations of territory in Belgium and Poland and the wholesale appropriation of British, Belgian and French territory in Africa. Fischer argued that this indicated that Germany was indeed embarked on a crusade for world domination and that this explained the apparent eagerness with which the German government embarked on war in August 1914. Not surprisingly, Fischer's work stirred up enormous controversy in Germany; indeed he was

---

9   AJP Taylor, *War by Timetable: how the First World War began* (London: Macdonald, 1972). He also put his theory across in his BBC lecture in the series *How Wars Begin* (BBC 1977).

10   Fritz Fischer, *Germany's Aims in the First World War* (New York: WW Norton, 1968).

The Fischer Thesis

ostracised by his colleagues, accused of treachery, and there is even evidence to suggest that attempts were made to tamper with the some of the archival material he had used.[11] His main critic, Professor Gerhard Ritter, argued that Fischer had been wrong to place so much emphasis on Riezler and that in any case a set of aims drawn up once war has started cannot be taken as proof of a country's intentions before the war, a point echoed more recently by Niall Ferguson.[12] Fischer, however, answered his critics in a second book, *War of Illusions*, which put forward evidence to suggest that Germany had been planning for war long before August 1914.

Fischer's thesis was enormously influential and it is still broadly accepted, with various modifications and acknowledgement of other factors, in academic circles outside Germany to this day. More recently, however, it has been criticised by the Cambridge historian Christopher Clark, who argued in *The Sleepwalkers* that the causation of the war was far too complex to allow for any country, Germany or anyone else, to be revealed as the 'murderer' à la Agatha Christie.[13] Moreover, whereas the Fischer thesis had implied that German expansionism was such a threat to European peace that it needed to be stopped, Clark argued that none of the issues exercising the statesmen and diplomats of 1914 were sufficiently weighty to be worth the war that actually ensued.

Fischer's main contention in *War of Illusions* was that Germany had been preparing well before 1914 for an aggressive war of conquest, that it certainly did want to initiate it and, whether or not

---

11   For the full story of the controversy over Fischer's thesis see Hartmut Pogge von Strandmann, 'The Political and Historical Significance of the Fischer Controversy,' *Journal of Contemporary History* 48:2 April 2013, 251-270.

12   Gerhard Ritter, 'Anti-Fischer: a new War Guilt thesis?' in Holger H. Herwig, *The Outbreak of World War I* 'Problems in European Civilization' series (Wadsworth Publishing, 1996); Niall Ferguson, The Pity of War, 1914-1918 (London: Penguin, 1999).

13   Christopher Clark, *The Sleepwalkers: how Europe went to war in 1914* (Allen Lane, 2011)

it was coincidence, German military planners had identified the spring or summer of 1914 as the optimum time at which to launch it, before the reforms in the Russian army rendered it too powerful for Germany to take on.[14] The documentary evidence of German war-planning is difficult to refute, and it is entirely consistent with the actual pattern of events in 1914, especially the ease with which the Kaiser issued his 'blank cheque' to Austria-Hungary. One of the most insistent voices encouraging the Austrians to take an intransigent line with the Serbs was von Moltke, the Chief of the General Staff. However, while there is a strong case that Germany willed war in 1914, knowing full well that it would become a general European war, it does not necessarily follow that Germany willed the *actual* war that broke out nor does it necessarily invalidate Germany's claim to have been acting defensively. The idea that Germany was fighting a defensive war might seem difficult to swallow, but Germany undoubtedly felt threatened by the growing power and ever-closer relationship of France and Russia and greatly feared the result of defeat by either of them. Moreover, the German High Command seems, however incredible we may find it, genuinely to have overlooked the likelihood of Britain's entering the war. The principle of the pre-emptive attack, 'getting your retaliation in first', was hardly new: the Boers had attacked British territory in 1899, not *vice versa* (and Japan was to do the same at Pearl Harbor in 1941) and attack is, after all, often accounted the best form of defence. The Germans may well have been fooling themselves, but it is not implausible that they genuinely believed they were fighting a defensive war and not a bid for European or world domination. This does not mean, of course, that they were right.

One difficulty in reaching a decision about Germany's responsibility for the war is that the concept of 'world domination' is not a well-defined one. The idea of a country or its leader plotting to dominate the world conjures up images either of a rather

---

14   Fritz Fischer, *War of Illusions: German policies, 1911-1914*, (London: Chatto and Windus, 1975).

The Fischer Thesis

simplistic view of Hitler's foreign policy or else of a James Bond villain. It is not necessary, however, to conquer a region in order to dominate it: Britain's extensive 'informal' empire was proof of that. The Germans could dominate Europe by their economic power and the spectacle of their military muscle without necessarily having to conquer all their neighbours. It was perfectly possible for the Germans to point out – as they often did – that the sort of world domination which they were accused of hankering after was almost exactly the sort of world domination already practised by their British and American opponents. It was also possible for them to argue that, given that Germany was by far the most economically productive and enterprising nation in Europe, German domination of Europe might not necessarily be a bad thing; similar arguments would be raised at the end of the century about Germany's dominant position within the European Union. Whether or not these arguments justify or excuse the invasion, conquest and brutal treatment of neutral Belgium and Luxembourg is, of course, a matter of opinion.

Were the Alliances to Blame?

A COMMONLY-HELD IDEA, often presented to school students, is that the European Great Powers were shackled together by their alliance system, so that when the first of them fell over the abyss into war, the others were all dragged down as well. It is an appealing image and is certainly easy to understand; unfortunately, it is wrong. *Not one* of the declarations of war by the Great Powers in July and August 1914 was the result of governments obeying the terms of an alliance. Germany was under no treaty obligation to stand by Austria-Hungary except in a defensive war, which the Serbian war clearly was not; Germany's support for Vienna was the product of the Kaiser and Bethmann Hollweg's issuing the famous 'blank cheque'. Russia and France were bound by their alliance to support each other, and Poincaré certainly reassured his hosts of French sympathy during his state visit to St Petersburg at height of the crisis; however, the French consistently went beyond the terms of their alliance with Russia in promising diplomatic and military support; when France did finally mobilise, however, it was not done in support of the Russians, but because the Germans had started to move against France itself. Italy was bound by its alliance to fight on the German side, but she held back and only entered the war the following year – on the allied side. Britain had no alliance with either France or Russia and clearly, to French fury, did not think itself bound by the 1904 entente to fight on France's side; indeed, it was only with difficulty that Britain agreed to uphold its own 1912 naval guarantee of the French coast. The only example of a long-standing treaty leading directly to a declaration of war was Britain's invoking of the 1839 Treaty of London that guaranteed the neutrality of Belgium and was reinforced in 1870 by bilateral treaties between Britain and France and between Britain and Prussia. Nevertheless, even this treaty, though requiring its signatories to guarantee and defend Belgium's independence, did not actually oblige any of them to declare war on any country that broke it. Britain's interest in defending Belgium was always primarily about protecting itself from invasion rather than humanitarian concern for the Belgians. The alliances certainly added to international tensions and laid down the parameters within which pre-1914 diplomacy was conducted, but the Great Powers did not simply follow their alliance partners into war, like some coach driver blindly following his satnav into a river: they carried far more direct responsibility than that.

Was the War Caused by Domestic Policy?

HISTORY IS FULL OF EXAMPLES of rulers who have embarked on what they hoped would be a short, victorious war in order to boost their standing at home: the Argentine invasion of the Falklands is a good example and similar accusations were made about US President Clinton's intervention in Kosovo at the height of the Monica Lewinski scandal. All the Powers that went to war in 1914 had significant domestic agendas which, to varying degrees, determined their readiness to seize the opportunity to go to war. In Germany, the government was increasingly worried about the apparently unstoppable rise of the Socialist Party (SPD), which by 1914 was the largest party in the Reichstag. Bethmann Hollweg hoped that patriotic support for a victorious war would rally working-class support for the regime and away from the SPD, although the socialists in fact proved enthusiastic supporters of the war once it broke out. In Russia the socialist threat was more overt: revolution had broken out in 1905, after Russia's defeat in the war with Japan, and the tsar had been forced to grant a form of constitution with an elected Duma. The threat of revolution had by no means receded after that, so the chance to stand by the Serbs in 1914 gave the tsar a very welcome opportunity to place himself at the head of his people and to ride a wave of popular patriotic fervour. The downside of this, of course, was that if the war went badly – as it did – the tsar would be vulnerable to a revolutionary backlash by those self-same people, as indeed happened. Austria-Hungary had its internal situation very much at the front of its mind in 1914: the Serb challenge threatened the integrity of the Dual Monarchy and Berchtold considered the possibility of incorporating Serbia into the Empire principally in order to provide a counter-weight within it to the Hungarians. France saw war in 1914 as an opportunity to put some of its deep political divisions behind it in the face of the German enemy: although the French had not precipitated the war, the kudos to be gained by liberating Alsace-Lorraine and avenging 1871 was too attractive to be missed. Britain too had significant domestic advantages to be gained from going to war: the opposing sides in Ireland, for example, who were busy arming for what looked set to be civil war, simply put their differences aside in 1914 and enlisted enthusiastically in the British army (though usually in different regiments). The extent to which these considerations actually *led* countries into war is less easy to judge: it is more likely that domestic considerations provided a compelling argument for opting for war once the diplomatic crisis had raised the possibility of it.

Why the First World War broke out

Conclusion

So, why did the First World War break out? It is not possible to identify one single reason, because in a sense we are not looking at one single war. No-one 'declared the First World War'; what happened in 1914 was the outbreak of four linked but separate conflicts: one between Austria-Hungary and Serbia, with which Russia was linked; a second between Germany and Russia; a third between Germany and France; and a fourth between Germany and Britain. Although it is clear that Germany was a common factor in three of these, Germany was not directly concerned in the conflict between Austria-Hungary and Serbia, which actually gave rise to the war. Each of these separate outbreaks of war had its own set of background factors, and none *actually* necessitated any of the others: it is just that in 1914 the statesmen acted as if they did.

Perhaps one way to consider the question is to ask who was actually working for peace rather than war in 1914. Only two characters stand out for their consistent efforts to contain the crisis and prevent it from catching fire: Sir Edward Grey, who sought to get the Austro-Serb issue referred to an international conference, and Lichnowsky, the German ambassador in London, who strove to avoid a rupture between Britain and Germany, but may inadvertently have done more harm than good by his misleadingly reassuring messages to Berlin. Grey has been criticised for not making it clearer until far too late in the day that Britain would stand by France, especially if Belgium were invaded. This is unfair: Grey could make no such announcement without the backing of the Cabinet and it was by no means sure until the very end that the Cabinet would have supported such a position. However, with hindsight it is possible to say that Grey was perhaps at fault in trying to act from a neutral, disinterested position when everyone knew where Britain's sympathies actually lay; it is conceivable that a more obviously partisan approach, such as Disraeli had taken against the Russians back in 1878, might have acted as a deterrent and lent more strength to Grey's calls for a conference.

If we now ask who was definitely working to provoke a war, we have no shortage of characters to choose from. From the start of the crisis the Austrian leaders, Berchtold and Conrad, were keen to push for war with Serbia, though they were less insistent on war with Russia. We should not forget the Serbs themselves, who had either planned, like Apis, or else, like Pasič, turned a blind eye to an assassination which they knew full well could provoke a war in the most sensitive and volatile region of the continent. It is very hard to absolve some of the Germans, especially Bethmann and Jagow, from blame for their conduct, not perhaps for eagerly seizing the opportunity for war, in which they were hardly alone, but for the cynicism of their deliberate attempts to undermine any alternative, more peaceful solution to the crisis. In this, however, they were no more guilty than others, notably Paléologue, misleading both the French and the Russian governments from his St Petersburg embassy, and the military chiefs in Berlin, Paris and St Petersburg, all of whom insistently pressed mobilisation in its fullest and most dangerous form on their governments: it is impossible not to be struck by the horror with which the German and Russian Chiefs of Staff responded to the idea that the process of mobilisation should be limited, halted or even reversed. It is only sensible for any state to have military contingency plans in the event of invasion or international crisis; however, Europe's Great Powers in 1914 had only one plan each, with no alternatives. The war plans (or even their railways' timetables) did not cause the war and did not even determine all the political and diplomatic decisions of those fateful summer days, but they did massively restrict the range of options open to statesmen who, on the whole, made no serious attempt to look further afield.

It is certainly possible to argue that no single country or individual should bear the blame for the war to the extent that Fritz Fischer alleges for Germany. The fact that the German High Command had identified the summer of 1914 as the optimum time for a war might mean that Germany took ready advantage of the July Crisis, but it certainly did not provoke it: Princip may have been right in his assertion that the Germans would still have found another way to provoke a war, but the case cannot be proved either way. What is clear is that no country planned or plotted for the war they actually got. Blame for the coming of war ought to be shared between the Austrians and Serbians, though not perhaps equally; the Russians may also be considered at fault, though they had good reasons for reacting as they did and they were in any case being to some extent misled by the French; 1914 was certainly not France's finest hour, even allowing for the bad luck that deprived it of two of its most influential anti-war voices, though it is probably guilty more of short-sighted negligence than of warmongering; Britain may be accused of adopting an unrealistic position, though it did at least propose peaceful solutions of a sort that had worked in the past and, *assuming that all parties preferred a peaceful solution to the alternative*, there was no reason to think they could not work again. The country that seemed most set not just on a war but on a *European* war was Germany. The Germans might have fooled themselves that Britain would stay out of it, though history suggested the exact opposite, and they may have assumed wrongly that the war would be short and decisive, but the fact remains that the Germans' only war plan entailed launching an attack on France, whether it had mobilised or declared war or not, and invading at least two neutral countries, Luxembourg and Belgium, whose integrity and

Conclusion

independence Germany had repeatedly guaranteed in writing. Later decades in the twentieth century would account the planning and launching of unprovoked war a war crime: it was one of the charges laid against the defendants at Nuremberg. If we allow the assassination as a valid reason for Austria's war with Serbia, Germany was the only country in 1914 which planned and carried out such an unprovoked attack, and perhaps for that reason alone, despite all the qualifications and other factors that historians have identified, Germany must bear the greatest responsibility for the catastrophe that engulfed Europe in August 1914.

Further Reading

THE CONTROVERSY OVER THE CAUSES of the First World is never likely to die down. All good accounts of the war carry a good summary of the issues relating to its outbreak, such as David Stevenson, *1914-1918: the history of the First World War* (London: penguin, 2005) or John Keegan, *The First World War* (London: Hutchinson, 1998). Ruth Henig's pamphlet *The Origins of the First World War* (Lancaster Pamphlets: London: Routledge, 2008) is a good way to start more specific reading on the topic, perhaps followed by Annika Mombauer's *The Origins of the First World War: Controversies and Consensus* (London: Longman, 2002) which offers a good overview of the debates that still rage on the topic. Fritz Fischer's *Germany's Aims in the First World War* (New York: WW Norton, 1968) is important reading, not least for anyone wanting to know what the fuss has all been about, while Christopher Clark's *The Sleepwalkers: how Europe went to war in 1914* (London: Allen Lane, 2011) is a masterly and wide-ranging narrative account which puts forward the view implicit in its title. Alan Palmer's *Twilight of the Habsburgs: The Life and Times of Emperor Francis Joseph* (Atlantic Monthly Press, 1997) tells the story from the point of view of 1914 most famous victim and places the Austro-Serbian stand-off in its longer-term context. Two classic accounts are still worth reading: George Malcolm Thomson's *The Twelve Days* written for the fiftieth anniversary of Sarajevo in 1964 is still a gripping account of the last days of peace (Hutchinson, 1964), while AJP Taylor's *War by Timetable: how the First World War began* (London: Macdonald, 1972) is a reminder of what a joy history can be when it is written by a master at the height of his game.

www.ingramcontent.com/pod-product-compliance
Lightning Source LLC
Chambersburg PA
CBHW051733040426
42447CB00008B/1113